RUDIMENTAL WA___ S

Skill-Strengthening Exercises for All Drummers

by Maria Martinez

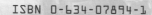

ISBN 0-634-07894-1

HAL•LEONARD® CORPORATION

7777 W. BLUEMOUND RD. P.O. BOX 13819 MILWAUKEE, WI 53213

Copyright © 2005 by HAL LEONARD CORPORATION
International Copyright Secured   All Rights Reserved

In Australia Contact:
Hal Leonard Australia Pty. Ltd.
22 Taunton Drive P.O. Box 5130
Cheltenham East, 3192 Victoria, Australia
Email: ausadmin@halleonard.com

Visit Hal Leonard Online at
www.halleonard.com

ABOUT THE AUTHOR

MARIA MARTINEZ, originally from Camaguey, Cuba and raised in New Orleans, Louisiana, is a respected drummer, percussionist, clinician, and educator now living and working in Los Angeles. She is the author of several educational publications, including *Brazilian Coordination for Drumset* and *Afro-Cuban Coordination for Drumset* (video and book/CD packages), and *Instant Guide to Drum Grooves* (book/CD package), all published by Hal Leonard.

Maria is a contributing author for *Modern Drummer, Percussive Notes, Drum Magazine, Latin Percussion Educational Newsletter*, and *Drum Instructors Only Newsletter.* She is co-founder and author of the "World Beat Rhythms (WBR) Beyond the Drum Circle" workshops and book/CD series, including *WBR–Brazil, WBR–Africa*, and *WBR–Cuba* (2003 Hal Leonard). Maria has taught master classes, conducted clinics, and played at events such as PASIC (Percussive Arts Society International Convention), NAMM (National Association of Music Merchants), TCAP (The California Arts Project), and the Berklee School of Music *World Percussion Festival*, among others.

Martinez pursues an active free-lance career, performing and sharing both stage and studio with such artists as Barry White, El Chicano, Rita Coolidge, Nel Carter, Angela Bofill, Klymaxx, Peach, Emmanuel, Johnny Paycheck, and Trini Lopez, among others. Her television and recording appearances include *The Late Show, The Drew Carey Show, Dukes of Hazzard, Soul Train, Desde Hollywood (Univision)*, and others.

Maria endorses Paiste Cymbals, Regal Tip Sticks, Latin Percussion, Pearl Drums, Remo Heads, E-Pad Company, and Rhythm Tech.

Professional Affiliations:
American Society of Composers, Authors, and Publishers (ASCAP)
American Federation of Musicians (AFM)
Percussive Arts Society (PAS)

Special Thanks to:
Robin Wright, Joe Porcaro, Jeff Schroedl, Rick Mattingly, Lori Hagopian, Frank Scarpelli, everyone at Hal Leonard, and my entire family for their love and support.

Thanks for Your Support:
Paiste: Rich Mangicaro, Andrew Shreve, Ed Clift, Steve Jacobs, Erik Paiste
Regal Tip: Carol Calato and Nick Mason
Remo: Brock Kaericher, Lane Davy, Matt Connors, Michelle Jacoby, Eduardo Chalo, Chris Hart, Roger Johnson
Latin Percussion: Steve Nigohosian, David McAllister, Terry Tlatelpa, Kimberly Redl, Memo Acevedo
Rhythm Tech: Spence Strand
E-Pad Company: Ed Eblen
Pearl: Jim Phiffer, Mike Farriss, Steve Armstrong
Mountain Rythym: Ryan Goldin
Sam Ash: Terry Bissette
The Music Trades: Richard Watson
Modern Drummer Publications: Bill Miller
LAUSD, Music Adviser: Steve Venz
Drum Tech: Tom Henry, Jim Carnelli

Equipment and Company Web sites:
Pearl Drums: www.pearldrum.com
Paiste: www.paiste.com
Latin Percussion: www.lpmusic.com
Remo: www.remo.com
Regal Tip: www.regaltip.com
E-pad: www.epadco.com
Mountain Rythym: www.mountainrhythm.com
Rhythm Tech: www.rhythmtech.com
Drum Tech: www.drumtech.com

Snare drum solos composed, arranged, and produced by Maria Martinez,
Sugar Cube (ASCAP) © 2004 All Rights Reserved.

Drums: Maria Martinez
Recorded, mixed, and mastered by Frank Scarpelli at QUIETSTREET STUDIOS, Hollywood, California.

TABLE OF CONTENTS

CD track   **Page**

1   Introduction   4

           About the Recording   4

           Chapter 1: Rudiments   5

2–41   Chapter 2: Flam Tap, Flamacue, and Paradiddle Variations   10

42–58   Chapter 3: Six Stroke Roll Variations   31

59–64   Chapter 4: Triple and Double Stroke Roll Variations   37

65–69   Chapter 5: Swiss Army Triple Variations   43

70–74   Chapter 6: Rolls, Tempos, and Rhythmic Pulsations   47

           Chapter 7: Let's Roll   50

75–82   Chapter 8: Rudimental Solos   59

           Equipment Used   69

INTRODUCTION 🔊

Track 1

Rudimental Warm-Ups is a book/CD package that explores warm-up exercises and variations based on the traditional twenty-six rudiments along with a number of drum corps, orchestral, European, and contemporary drum rudiments. This book offers an exciting and different approach to learning the warm-up variations based on the traditional rudiments and is a great tool for drum students of all levels and music educators who are teaching students to have a deeper knowledge of rudiments and rhythmic phrasing.

Drumset players will find new and challenging ways to play the rudiments and variations. Once comfortable with the stickings, the drumset player can choose one of the bass drum and hi-hat ostinatos to play underneath the exercises. These ostinatos will help drummers focus on coordination while sharpening technique and rhythmic vocabulary. The student is encouraged to play the alternate stickings provided below every exercise in the book. In addition, important *hints* are offered throughout the book to help drummers successfully accomplish the goal of playing each exercise.

The CD provides an opportunity to listen and play along while giving the student an interactive way to learn the rudimental variations. Each audio example will allow the student to listen and practice the exercises along with specific instructions on techniques used to play each exercise. The book also contains a few photographs for visual aid with technical instruction.

Much like scales are to a guitarist, the rudiments are an important learning tool designed to further the drummer's rhythmic vocabulary, control, and technique. This book provides many different ways to learn, practice, and master the rudiments, and with patience and dedication, it will also promote musical creativity and drastically expand one's rhythmic universe.

ABOUT THE RECORDING

In order to assist you in developing the *Rudimental Warm-Ups* covered in this book, the accompanying CD features demonstrations and play-along tracks. These tracks will give you the opportunity to learn and practice the examples in an interactive fashion. For the exercises, most examples are performed in the following fashion: The examples are played, followed by empty measures of click track for the student to echo the demonstration. This process then repeats (performance then click track). The student is encouraged to try different combinations of phrasings during these empty click tracks. The demonstrations on the CD are identified with the corresponding audio icons 🔊 next to the written example. Track 1 is the audio introduction, listen to it now to get started on your *Rudimental Warm-Ups!*

CHAPTER 1: Rudiments

The Percussive Arts Society International Drum Rudiments consist of the traditional twenty-six rudiments along with a number of drum corps, orchestral, European, and contemporary drum rudiments.

Practice Suggestions

Practice each rudiment at a slow tempo. Once you're comfortable with the sticking, increase the tempo and then slow back down to the original starting point before moving to the next rudiment. Another way to practice these rudiments (especially those that trouble you the most) is by utilizing a metronome and an egg timer. This approach requires record-keeping and more discipline, but within a few days the benefits will be very noticeable. First, play the rudiment at a comfortable tempo, use the metronome to determine the beats per minute (bpm), and write it down for future reference. Next, increase the tempo on the metronome by one click and play the rudiment continuously for at least two minutes. (Use the egg timer to help you keep track of time.) When you begin your next practice session, start with the same metronome setting that you ended your previous session with (or one click slower) to maintain consistency and forward momentum. As long as the rudiment is being played with accuracy you can continue to increase the tempo by one click over a period of days or weeks. Eventually you can expect to spend more time playing a particular rudiment at the same tempo before being able to increase it, but don't feel discouraged. Instead, refer to your records so you can appreciate the progress you've made since you first started.

Hints

- Do not sacrifice accuracy for speed.

- It is very important to watch your hands and stick height while practicing rudiments, so practice in front of a mirror whenever possible.

- Play all unaccented notes about a quarter inch from the snare head and play accents using full strokes.

- Stick tips should make a straight up and down motion. Watch the tip of the stick to determine the correct motion.

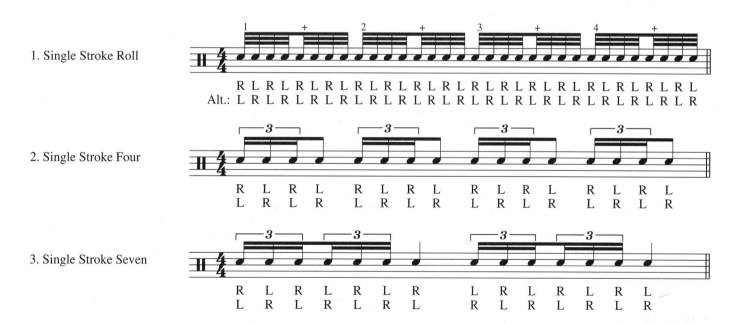

Reprinted by permission of the Percussive Arts Society, Inc.,
701 NW Ferris, Lawton, OK 73507-5442; E-mail:
percarts@pas.org; Web: www.pas.org

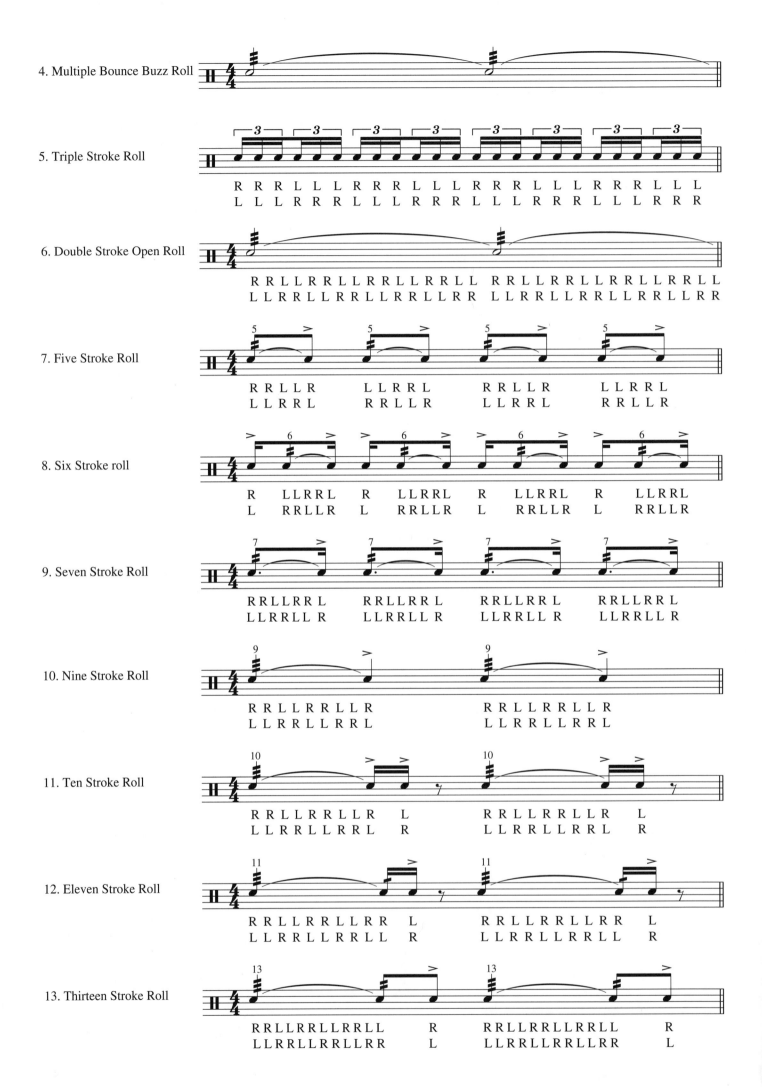

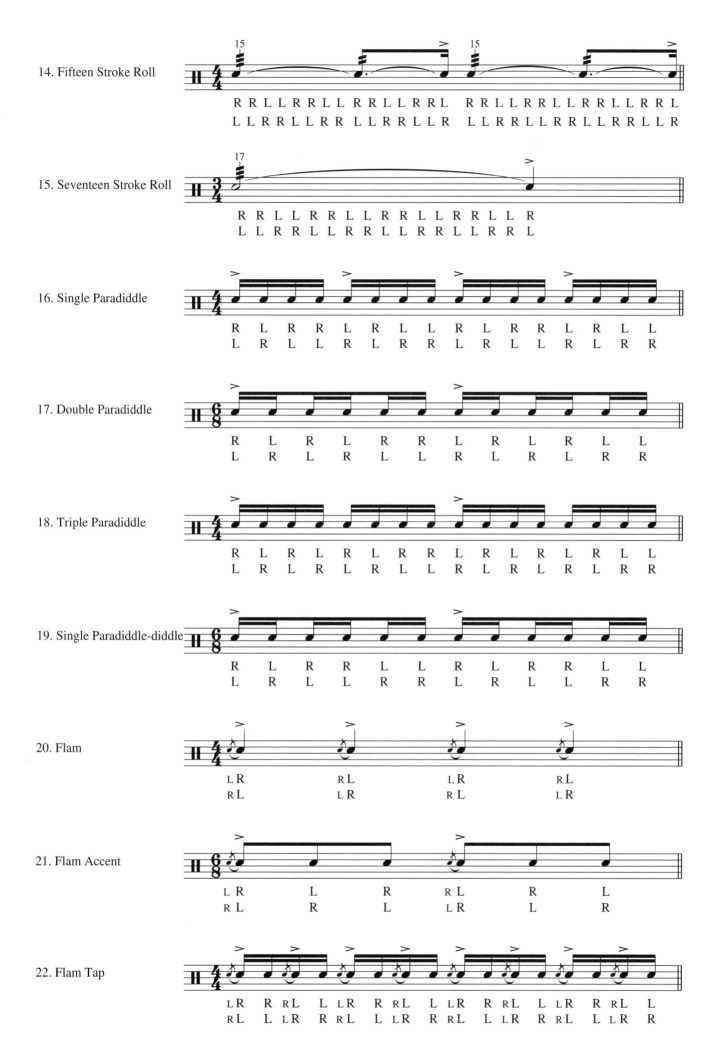

14. Fifteen Stroke Roll

15. Seventeen Stroke Roll

16. Single Paradiddle

17. Double Paradiddle

18. Triple Paradiddle

19. Single Paradiddle-diddle

20. Flam

21. Flam Accent

22. Flam Tap

CHAPTER 2:
Flam Tap, Flamacue, and Paradiddle Variations

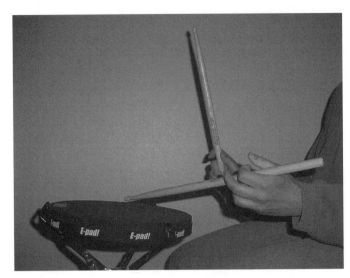

Right Hand Flam

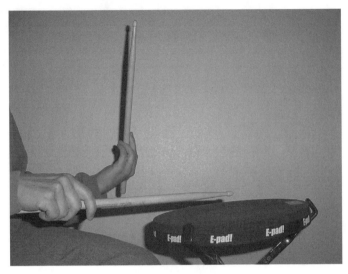

Left Hand Flam

The following examples are variations based on the *flam tap, flamacue,* and *paradiddle* rudiments. These rudimental variations consist of flams with single, duple, and triple sticking combinations. Utilize a metronome and/or tap your foot as you repeat each exercise until you feel comfortable with the sticking.

The flam offers a fuller sound by reinforcing a main note with a grace note. The correct stick position is crucial to successfully playing the flam rudiment. The photographs illustrate the correct starting stick positions for playing the right hand and left hand flam rudiment.

Hints

- The grace note should be about a quarter inch (not more than one inch) off the surface of the snare head.

- The position of the main note should begin in an up position (about twelve inches) to allow a full down stroke motion.

- Do not strike the sticks at the same exact time. Instead, strike the grace note slightly before the single note that follows.

- You should never hear two separate distinct notes played; it should be one full sounding stroke.

- Never lift your arms. Use full wrist strokes only.

- Watch your sticks or use a mirror during practice.

- When alternating the flam rudiment, match the height and motion of the previous flam.

- To build stamina, practice playing the warm-ups with brushes instead of sticks.

Exercises

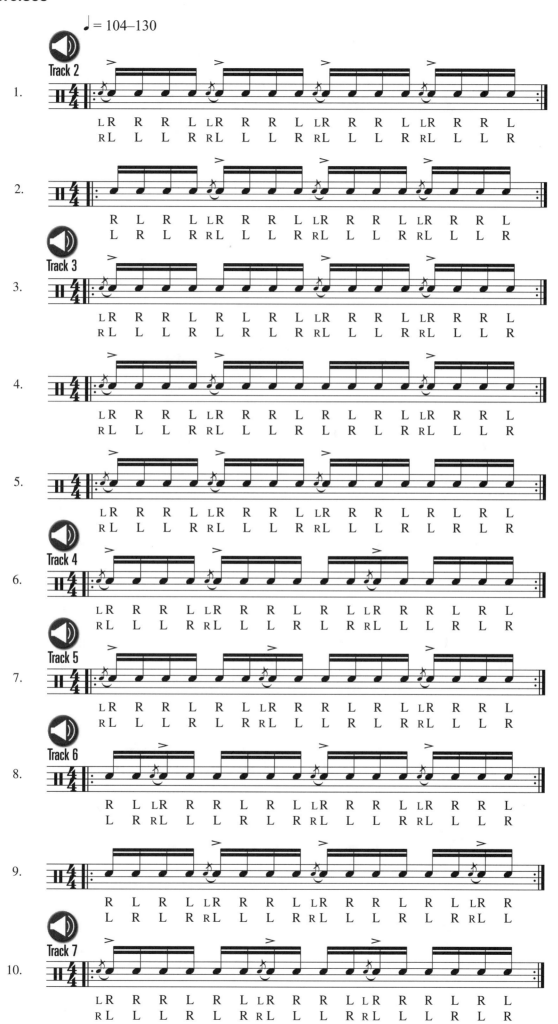

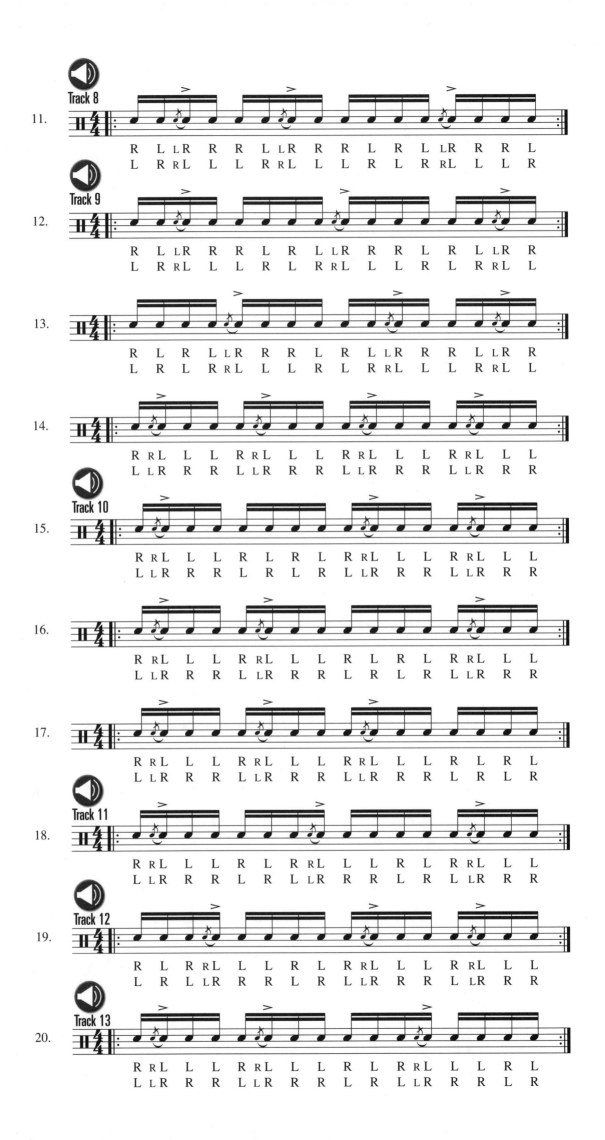

Four-bar Phrases

The four-bar exercises are combined phrases based on the flam tap, flamacue, and paradiddle rudimental variations. Repeat each phrase until you are comfortable with the different sticking combinations, and then create your own four-bar phrases.

A.

```
L R  R  R  L L R  R  R  L R L R L L R  R  R L    L R  R  R  L L R  R  R L R L R L L R  R  R L
R L  L  L  L R r L  L  L  L R L R L R r L  L  L R    r L  L  L  L R r L  L  L  L R L R L R r L  L  L R
```

```
L R  R  R  L L R  R  R  L R L L R  R  R L R L    L R  R  R  L L R  R  R L R L L R  R  R L R L
R L  L  L  L R r L  L  L  L R L R r L  L  L R L R    r L  L  L  L R r L  L  L  L R L R r L  L  L R L R
```

B.

```
L R  R  R  L L R  R  R  L L R  R  R  L L R  R  R L    L R  R  R  L L R  R  R L L R  R  R L L R  R  R L
R L  L  L  L R r L  L  L  L R r L  L  L  L R r L  L  L R    r L  L  L  L R r L  L  L  L R r L  L  L  L R r L  L  L R
```

```
R L  R  R r L  L  L  R L R L R r L  L  L  L R r L  L  L L    R L  R r L  L  L  L R L R r L  L  L  L R r L  L  L
L R  L L r R  R  R  L R L L r R  R  R  L L r R  R    L R  L L r R  R  R  L R L L r R  R  R  L L r R  R  R
```

C.

```
L R  R  R  L L R  R  R  L L R  R  R  L R L R L    L R  R  R  L L R  R  R L L R  R  R L R L R L
R L  L  L  L R r L  L  L  L R r L  L  L  L R L R L R    r L  L  L  L R r L  L  L  L R r L  L  L R L R L R
```

```
R r L  L  L  L R r L  L  L  L R L R r L  L  L  L R L    R r L  L  L  L R r L  L  L  L R L R r L  L  L  L R L
L L r R  R  R  L L r R  R  R  L R L L r R  R  R  L R    L L r R  R  R  L L r R  R  R  L R L L r R  R  R  L R
```

13

D.

LR R R L R L LR R R L LR R R L R L   LR R R L R L LR R R L LR R R L R L
RL L L R L R RrL L L R L L L L R   RL L L R L R RrL L L L R L L L R

RrL L L R L RrL L L R L RrL L L   RrL L L R L RrL L L R L RrL L L
L LR R R L R L LR R R L R LLR R R   L LR R R L R LLR R R L R LLR R R

E.

R L LR R R L R L LR R R LLR R R L   R L LR R R L R L LR R R LLR R R L
L R RrL L L R L R RrL L L R RrL L L R   L R RrL L L R L R RrL L L R RrL L L R

RrL L L RrL L L R L R L RrL L L   RrL L L RrL L L R L R L RrL L L
L LR R R L LR R R L R L R LLR R R   L LR R R L LR R R L R L R LLR R R

F.

R L LR R R L LR R R L R L LR R R L   R L LR R R L LR R R L R L LR R R L
L R RrL L L R RrL L L R L R RrL L L R   L R RrL L L R RrL L L R L R RrL L L R

LR R R L R L LR R R L R L LR R R L   LR R R L R L LR R R L R L LR R R L
RL L L R L R RrL L L R L R RrL L L R   RL L L R L R RrL L L R L R RrL L L R

G.

RrL L L R L R L RrL L L RrL L L   RrL L L R L R L RrL L L RrL L L
L LR R R L R L R L LR R R L LR R R   L LR R R L R L R L LR R R L LR R R

LR R R L LR R R L R L R L LR R R L   LR R R L LR R R L R L R L LR R R L
RL L L R RrL L L R L R L RrL L L R   RL L L R RrL L L R L R L RrL L L R

H.

R L L R R R L R L L R R R L R L L R   R L L R R R L R L L R R R L R L L R
L R rL L L R L R rL L L L R L R rL L   L L R rL L L R L R rL L L L R L R rL L

R L R L L R R R L L R R R L L R R R L   R L R L L R R R L L R R R L L R R R L
L R L R rL L L R rL L L L R rL L L R   L R L R rL L L R rL L L L R rL L L R

I.

R L R L L R R R L R L L R R R L L R R   R L R L L R R R L R L L R R R L L R R
L R L R rL L L R L R rL L L L R rL L   L R L R rL L L R L R rL L L L R rL L

R L L R R R L L R R R L R L L R R R L   R L L R R R L L R R R L R L L R R R L
L R rL L L L R rL L L R L R rL L L R   L R rL L L L R rL L L R L R rL L L R

J.

R L R L L R R R L L R R R L R L L R R   R L R L L R R R L L R R R L R L L R R
L R L R rL L L L R rL L L L R L R rL L   L R L R rL L L L R rL L L L R L R rL L

R rL L L L R rL L L L R rL L L L R rL L L   R rL L L L R rL L L L R rL L L L R rL L L
L L R R R L L R R R L L R R R L L R R R   L L R R R L L R R R L L R R R L L R R R

Eight-bar Phrases

The eight-bar exercises are combined phrases based on the flam tap, flamacue, and paradiddle rudimental variations. Repeat each phrase until you are comfortable with the different sticking combinations, and then create your own eight-bar phrases.

Track 14

A.

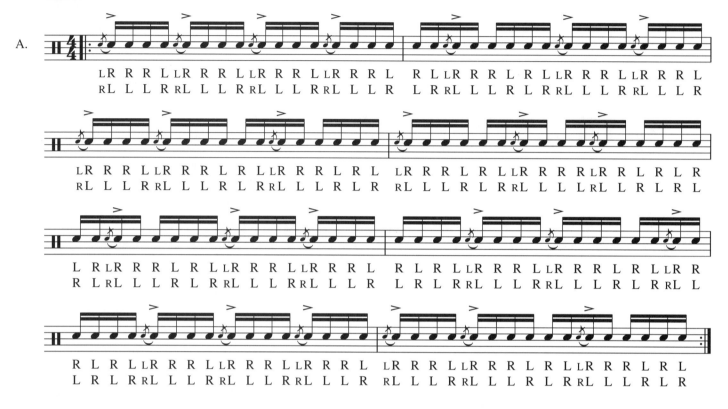

B.

Exercises

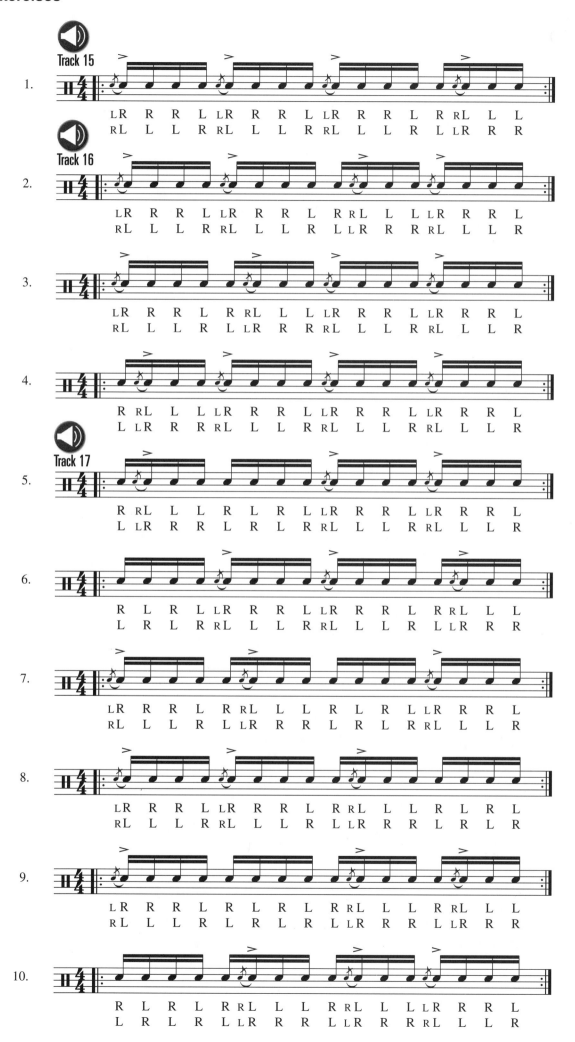

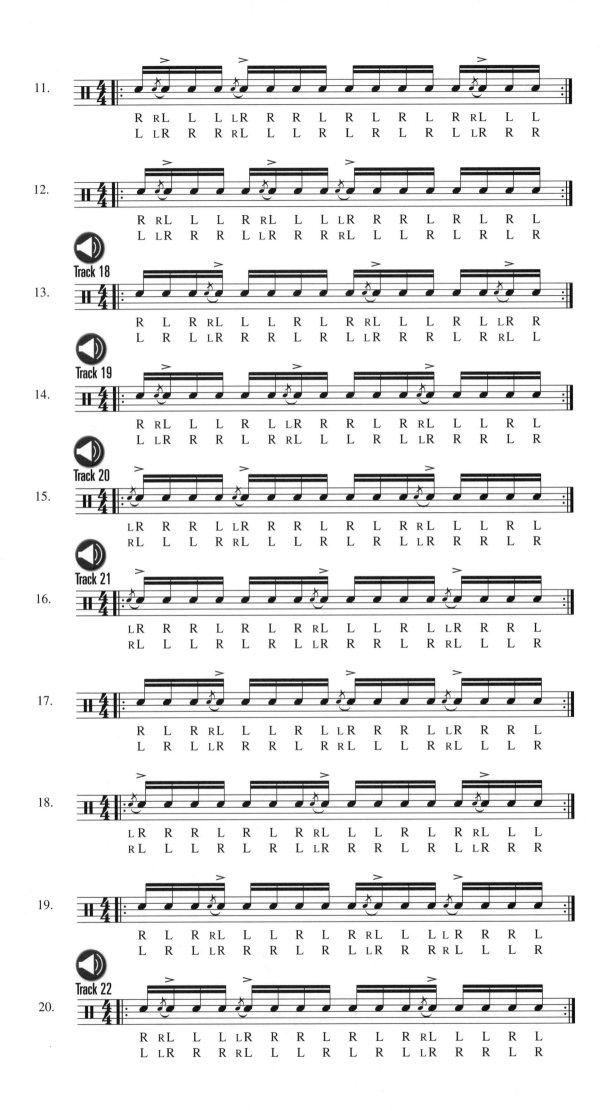

Four-bar Phrases

The four-bar exercises are combined phrases based on the flam tap, flamacue, and paradiddle rudimental variations. Repeat each phrase until you are comfortable with the different sticking combinations, and then create your own four-bar phrases.

A.

R RL L LLR R LLR R LLR R L   R RL L LLR R LLR R LLR R L
LLR R RRL L L RRL L L RRL L L R   LLR R RRL L L RRL L L RRL L L R

LR R R L R L R RL L L R L RRL L L   LR R R L R L RRL L L R L RRL L L
RL L L R L R LLR R R L R RRLR R R   RL L L R L R LLR R R L R LLR R R

Track 23

B.

LR R R LLR R R L RRL L LLR R R L   LR R R LLR R R L RRL L LLR R R L
RL L L RRL L L R LLR R RRL L L R   RL L L RRL L L R LLR R RRL L L R

R L RRL L L R L RRL L LLR R R L   R L RRL L L R L RRL L LLR R R L
L R LLR R R L R LLR R RRL L L R   L R LLR R R L R LLR R RRL L L R

C.

LR R R LLR R R LLR R R L RRL L L   LR R R LLR R R LLR R R L RRL L L
RL L L RRL L L RRL L L R LLR R R   RL L L RRL L L RRL L L R LLR R R

RRL L L R LLR R R L RRL L L L R L   RRL L L R LLR R R L RRL L L L R L
LLR R R L RRL L L R LLR R R L R   LLR R R L RRL L L R LLR R R L R

D.

LR R R L R L R L RRL L L RRL L L   LR R R L R L R L RRL L L RRL L L
RL L L R L R L R LLR R R LLR R R   RL L L R L R L R LLR R R LLR R R

R RL L LLR R R L R L RRL L L L R L   R RL L LLR R R L R L RRL L L L R L
LLR R RLL L L R L R L RLLR R R L R   LLR R RRL L L R L R L LLR R R L R

E.

R L R LLR R R LLR R R L RRL L L   R L R LLR R R LLR R R L RRL L L
L R L RRL L L RRL L L R LLR R R   L R L RRL L L RRL L L R L LLR R R

R L R RL L L R L R L RRL L L L R LLR R   R L RRL L L R L R L RRL L L L R LLR R
L R L LLR R R L R L R LLR R R L RRL L   L R L LLR R R L R L R L R L RRL L

19

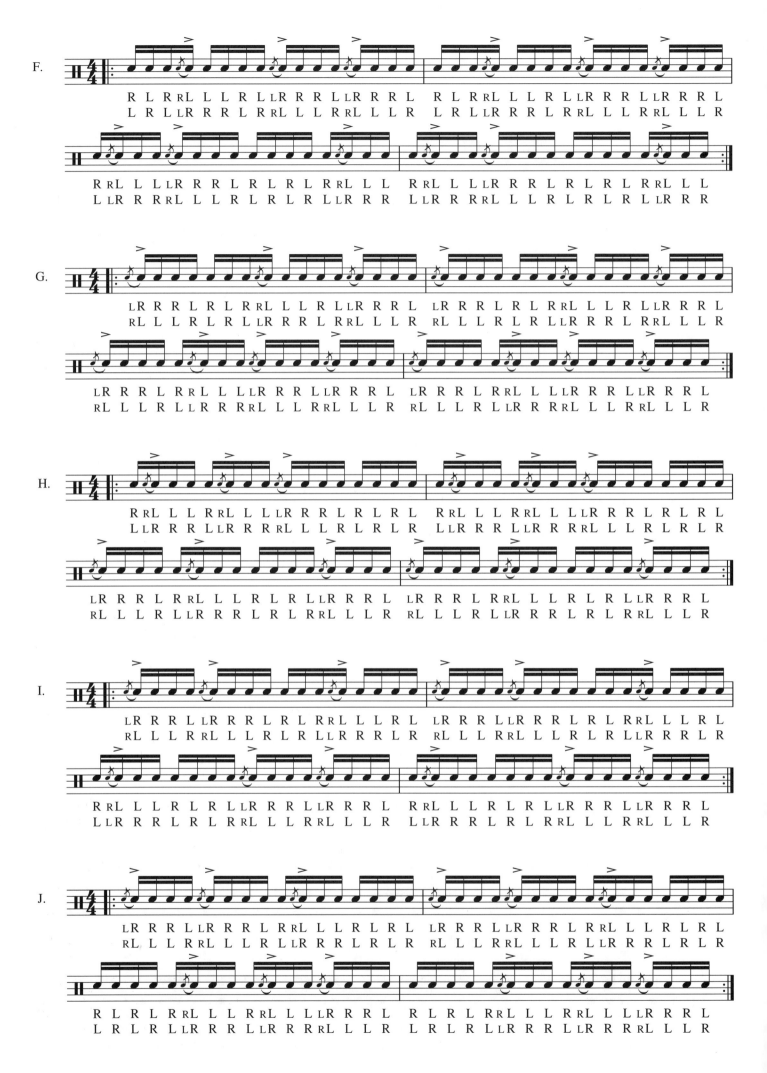

Eight-bar Phrases

The eight-bar exercises are combined phrases based on the flam tap, flamacue, and paradiddle rudimental variations. Repeat each phrase until you are comfortable with the different sticking combinations, and then create your own eight-bar phrases.

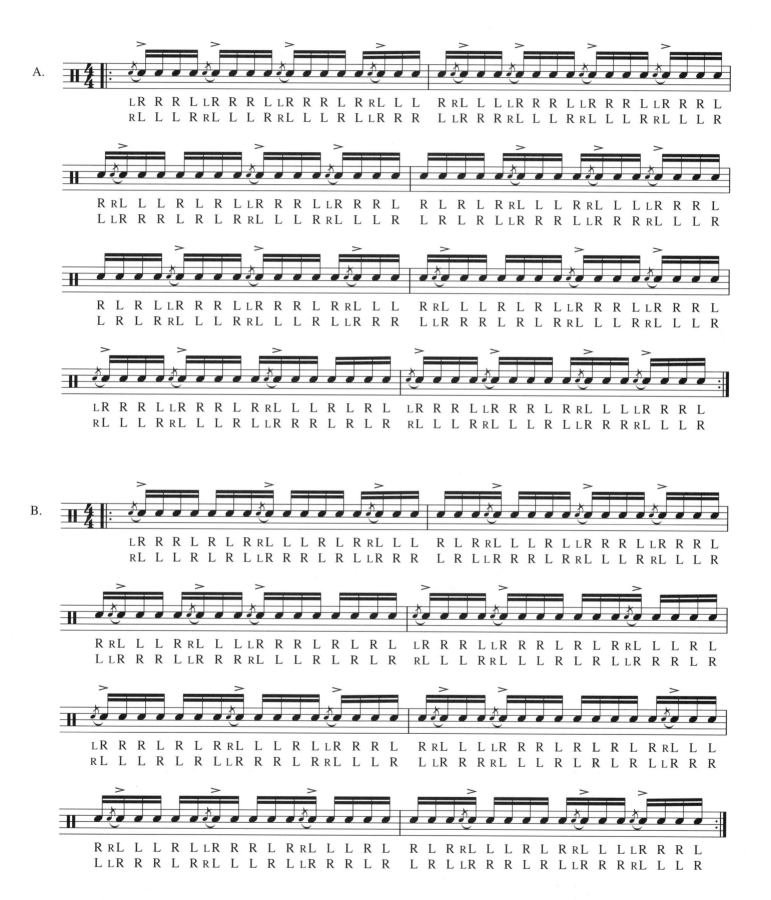

Exercises

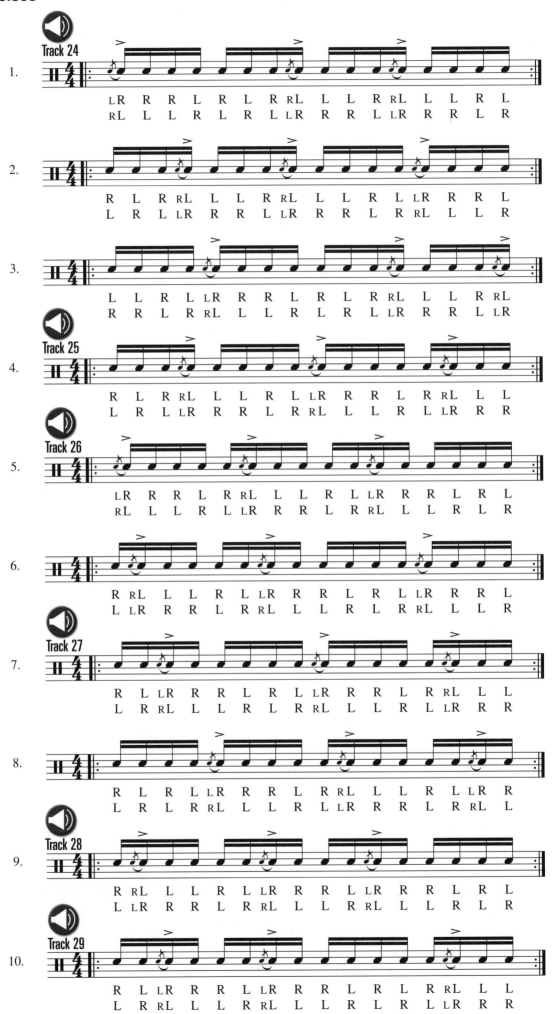

22

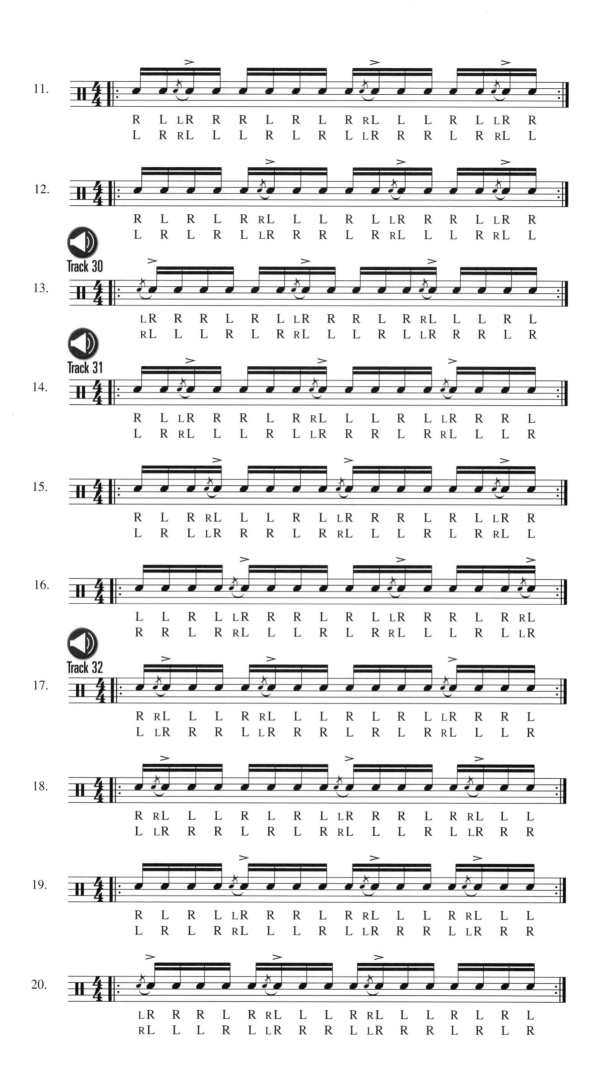

Four-bar Phrases

The four-bar exercises are combined phrases based on the flam tap, flamacue, and paradiddle rudimental variations. Repeat each phrase until you are comfortable with the different sticking combinations, and then create your own four-bar phrases.

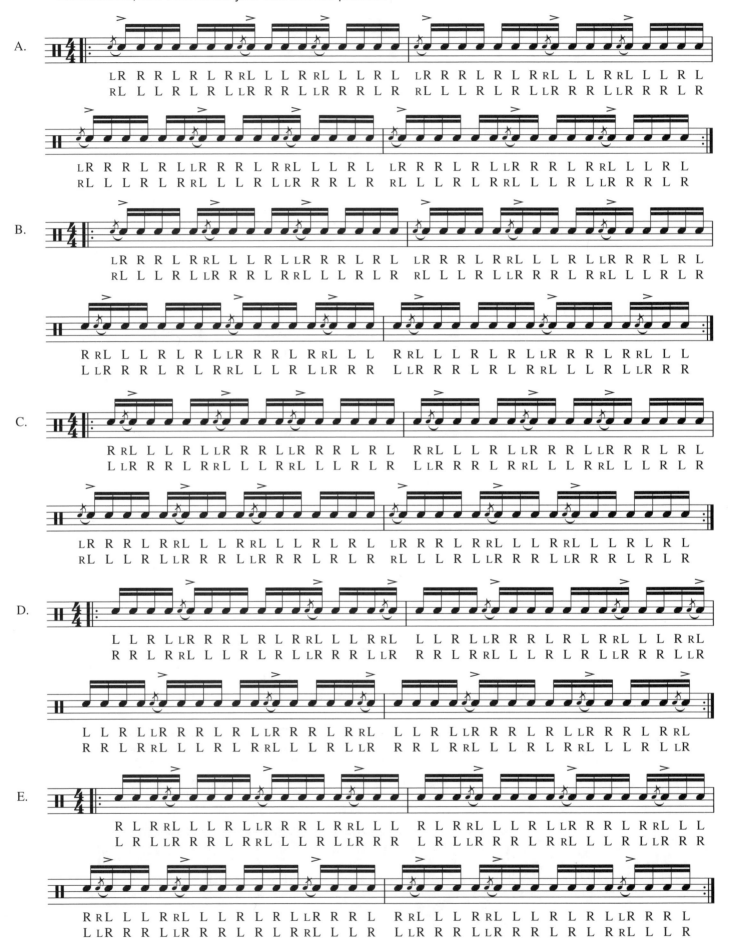

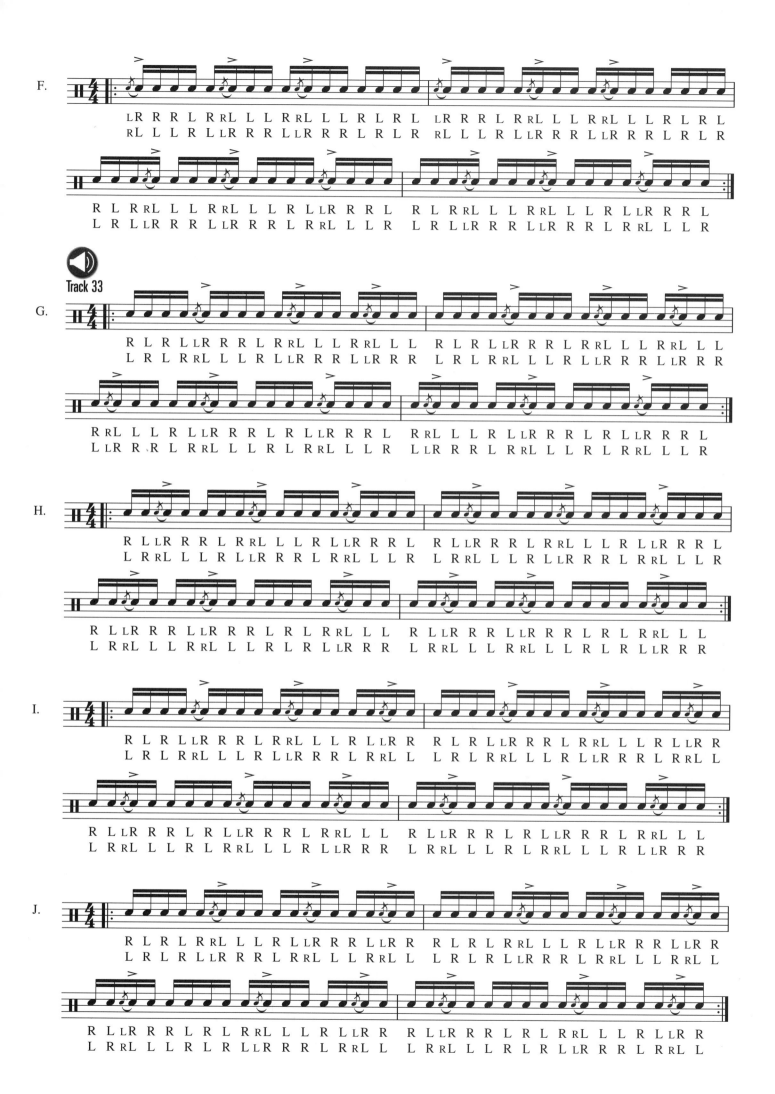

Eight-bar Phrases

The eight-bar exercises are combined phrases based on the flam tap, flamacue, and paradiddle rudimental variations. Repeat each phrase until you are comfortable with the different sticking combinations, and then create your own eight-bar phrases.

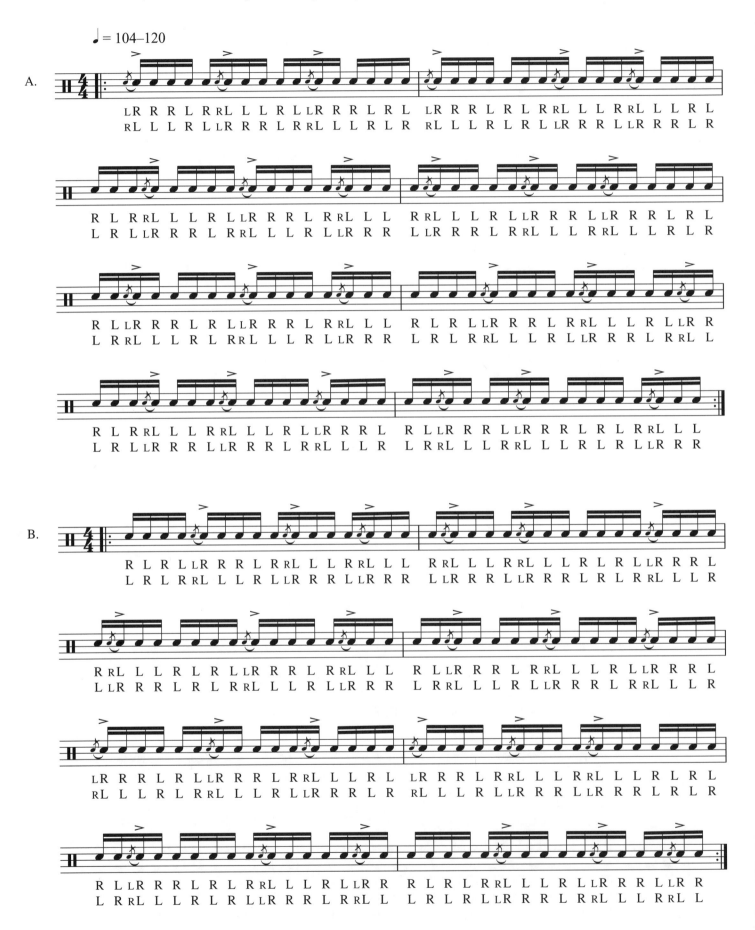

Exercises

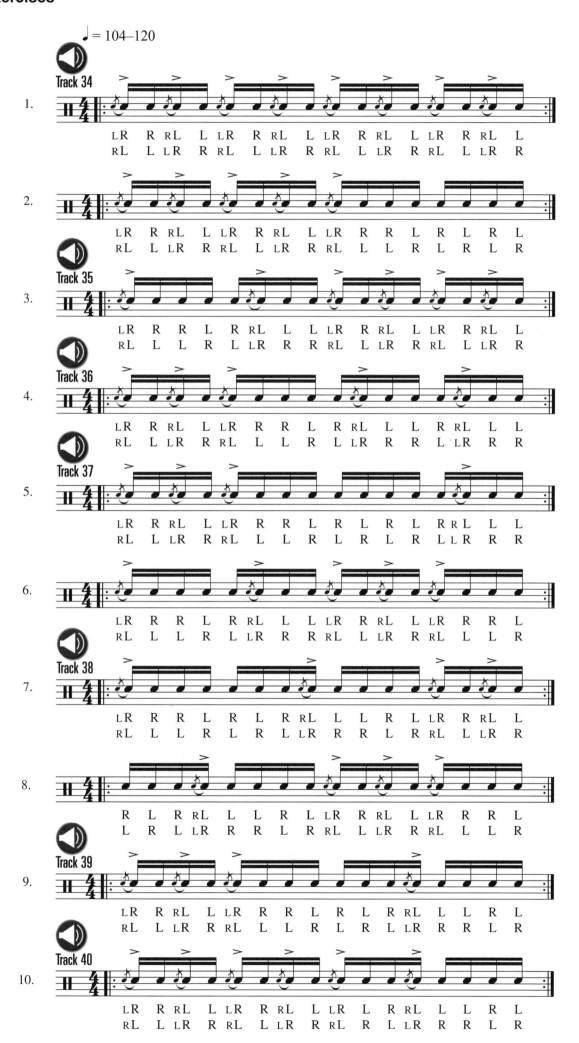

27

Four-bar Phrases

The four-bar exercises are combined phrases based on the flam tap, flamacue, and paradiddle rudimental variations. Repeat each phrase until you are comfortable with the different sticking combinations, and then create your own four-bar phrases.

Eight-bar Phrases

The eight-bar exercises are combined phrases based on the flam tap, flamacue, and paradiddle rudimental variations. Repeat each phrase until you are comfortable with the different sticking combinations, and then create your own eight-bar phrases.

Bass Drum and Hi-hat Ostinatos

The following bass drum and hi-hat ostinatos can be played underneath the previous flam tap, flamacue, and paradiddle rudimental exercises.

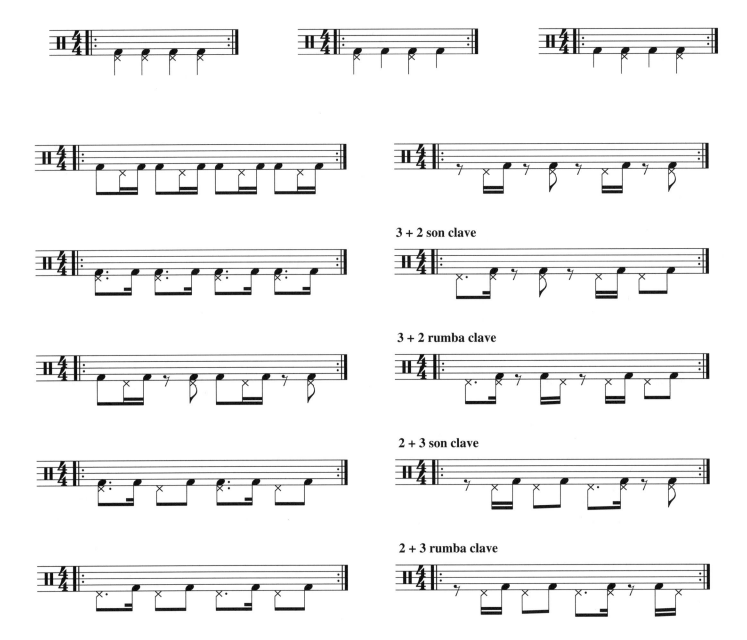

3 + 2 son clave

3 + 2 rumba clave

2 + 3 son clave

2 + 3 rumba clave

CHAPTER 3:
Six Stroke Roll Variations

The following examples are variations based on the *six stroke roll* rudiment. These rudimental variations consist of single and duple sticking combinations. It is very important to watch your hands and stick height while practicing these variations. Remember to play all unaccented notes about a quarter inch from the snare head and play all accents using full strokes. Utilize a metronome and/or tap your foot as you repeat each exercise until you feel comfortable with the sticking.

Exercises

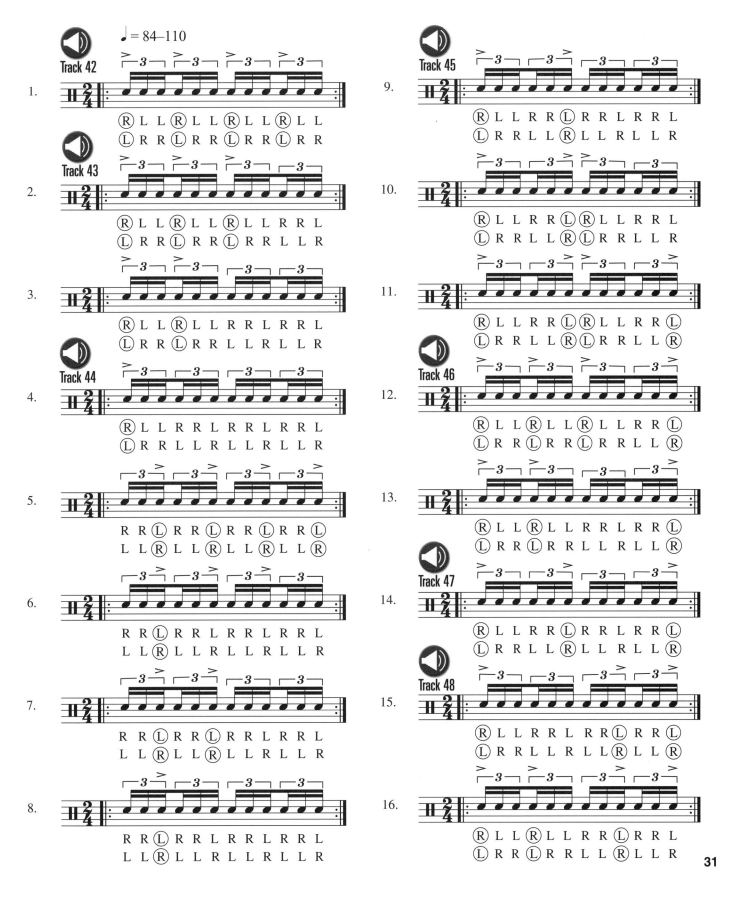

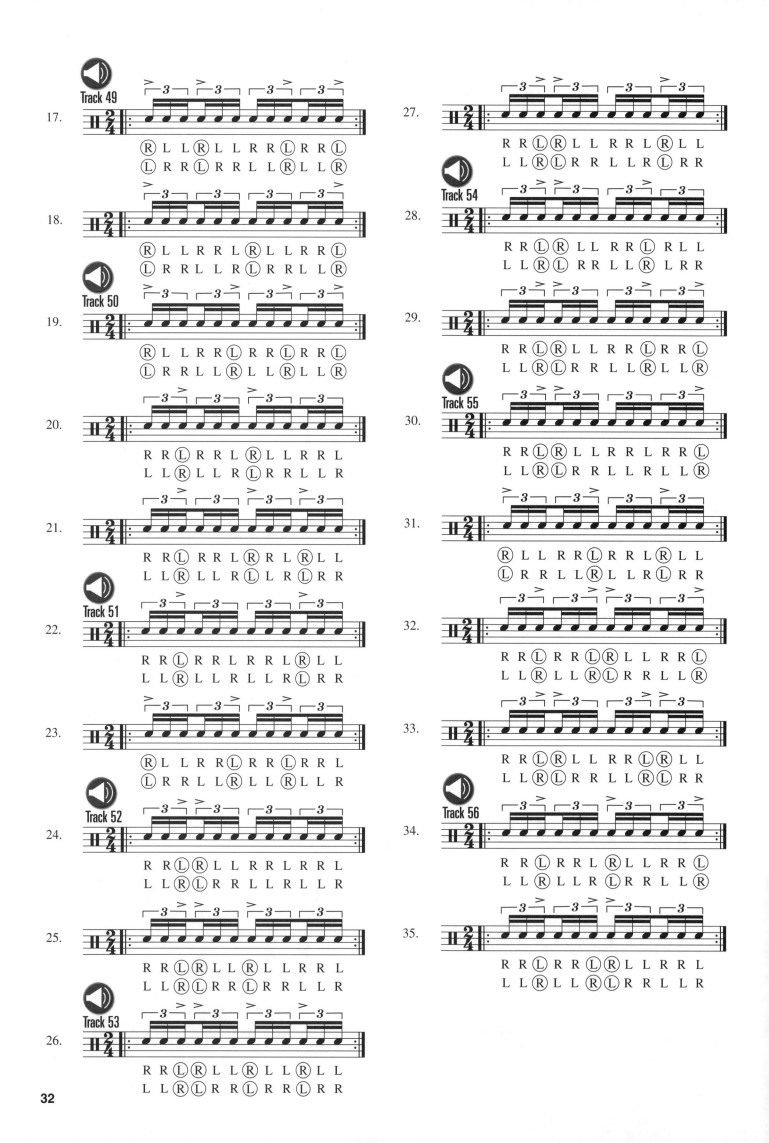

Four-bar Phrases

The four-bar exercises are combined phrases based on the six stroke roll rudimental variations. Repeat each phrase until you are comfortable with the different sticking combinations, and then create your own four-bar phrases.

E.

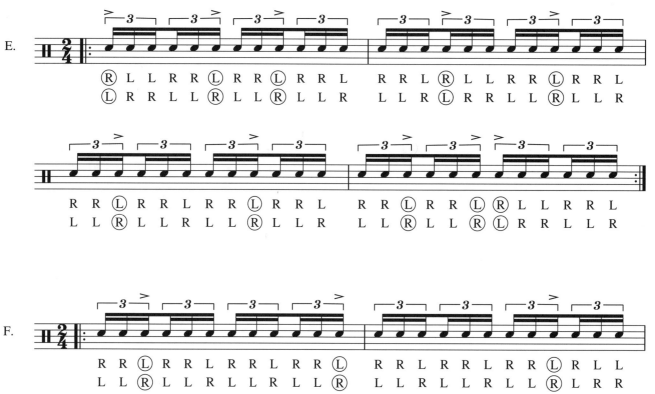

R L L R R L R R L R R L   R R L R L L R R L R R L
L R R L L R L L R L L R   L L R L R R L L R L L R

F.

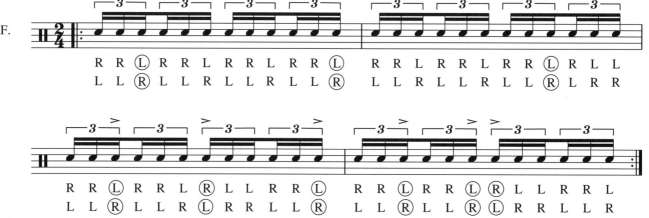

R R L R R L R R L R R L   R R L R R L R R L R L L
L L R L L R L L R L L R   L L R L L R L L R L R R

R R L R R L R L L R R L   R R L R R L R L L R R L
L L R L L R L R R L L R   L L R L L R L R R L L R

Eight-bar Phrases

The eight-bar exercises are combined phrases based on the six stroke roll rudimental variations. Repeat each phrase until you are comfortable with the different sticking combinations, and then create your own eight-bar phrases.

♩ = 84–110

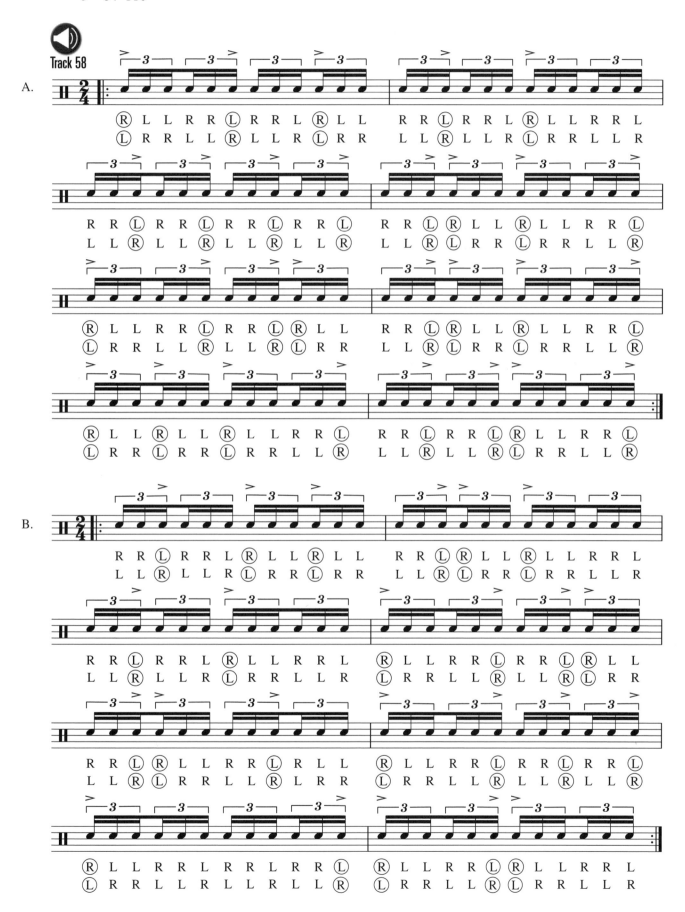

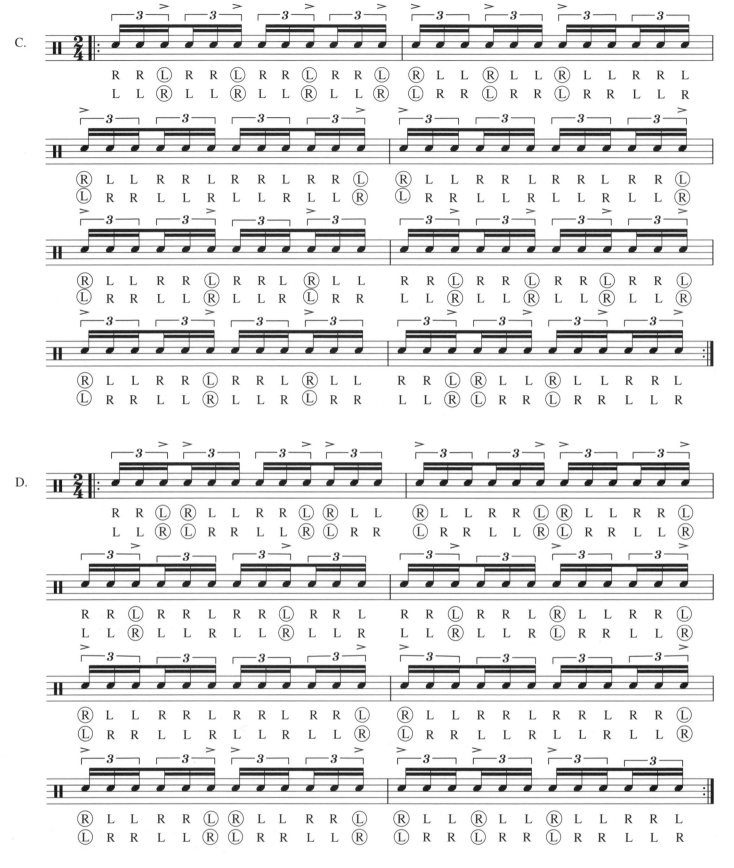

Bass Drum and Hi-hat Ostinatos

The following bass drum and hi-hat ostinatos can be played underneath the previous six stroke roll rudimental exercises.

CHAPTER 4: Triple and Double Stroke Roll Variations

The following examples are variations based on the *triple* and *double stroke roll* rudiments. These rudimental variations consist of duple and triple sticking combinations. Utilize a metronome and/or tap your foot as you repeat each exercise until you feel comfortable with the sticking.

Exercises

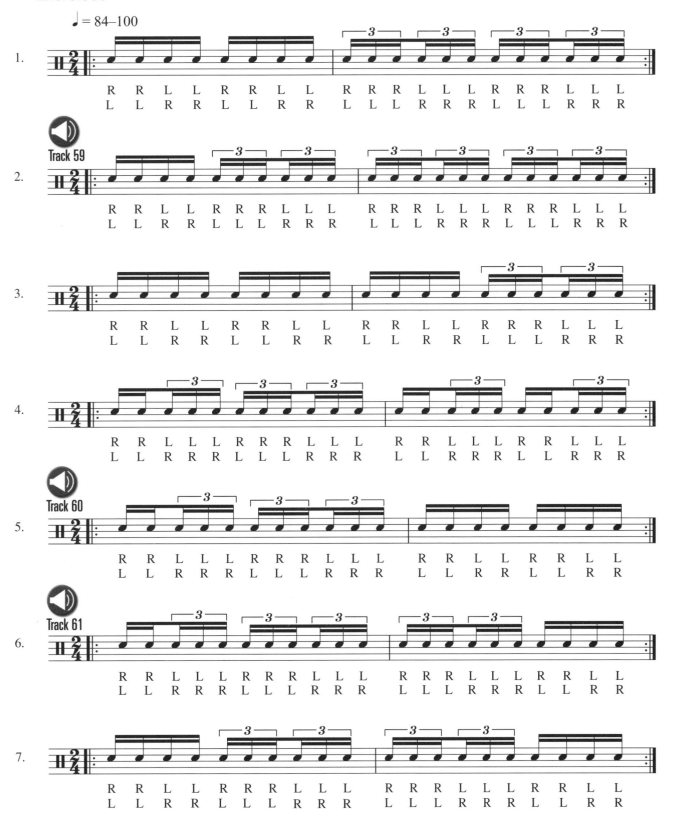

Track 62

8.

R R L L L L R R L L L
L L L R R R L L L R R R

R R L L R R L L
L L R R L L R R

9.

R R L L R R L L
L L R R L L R R

R R R L L R R L L
L L L R R L L R R

10.

R R L L L R R L L
L L L R R R L L R R

R R L L R R L L
L L R R L L R R

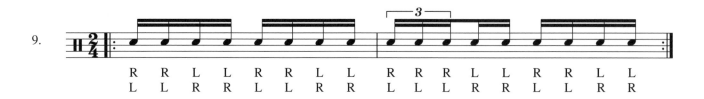

11.

R R R L L L R R L L
L L L R R R L L R R

R R L L R R R L L L
L L R R L L L R R R

12.

R R L L L R R R L L L
L L L R R R L L L R R R

R R R L L L R R R L L
L L L R R R L L L R R

13.

R R R L L R R L L
L L L R R L L R R

R R L L R R L L
L L R R L L R R

14.

R R R L L R R R L L L
L L L R R L L L R R R

R R L L R R R L L
L L R R L L L R R

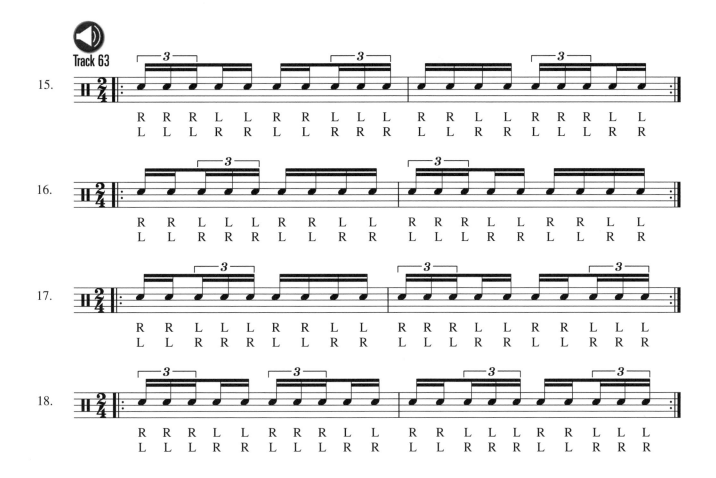

15. R R R L L L R R R L L L R R L L L R R R L L L
    L L L R R R L L L R R R L L L R R R L L L R R

16. R R L L L R R L L R R L L L R R L L L
    L L R R R L L L R R L L L R R R L L R R

17. R R L L L R R L L R R R L L L R R L L L
    L L R R R L L R R L L L R R L L R R R

18. R R R L L L R R R L L L R R L L L R R R L L L L
    L L L R R R L L L R R R L L R R R L L R R R

Four-bar Phrases

The four-bar exercises are combined phrases based on the triple and double stroke roll rudimental variations. Repeat each phrase until you are comfortable with the different sticking combinations, and then create your own four-bar phrases.

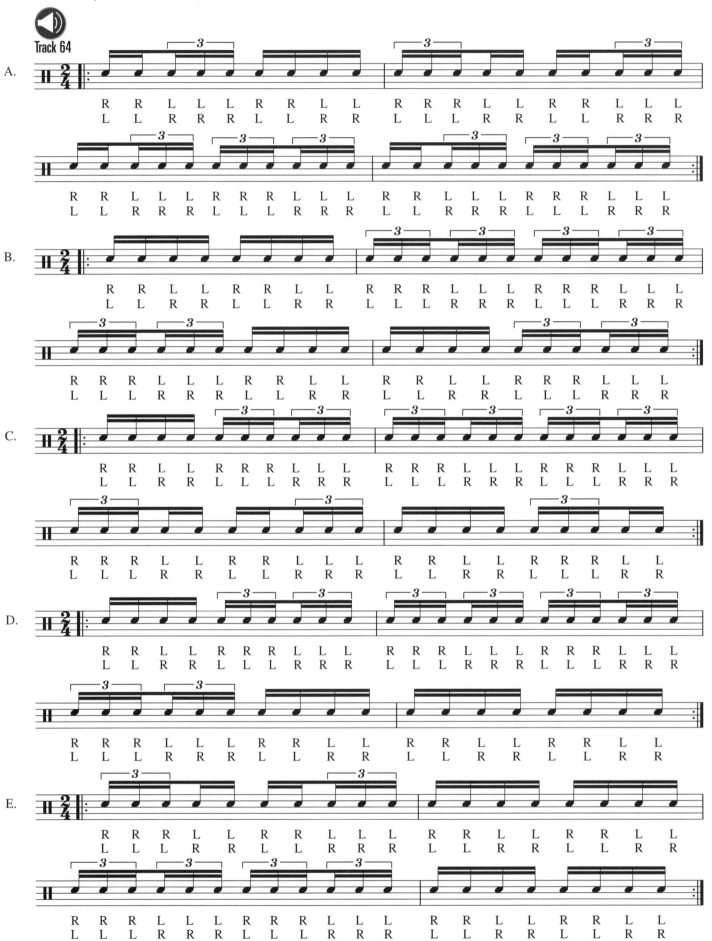

Track 64

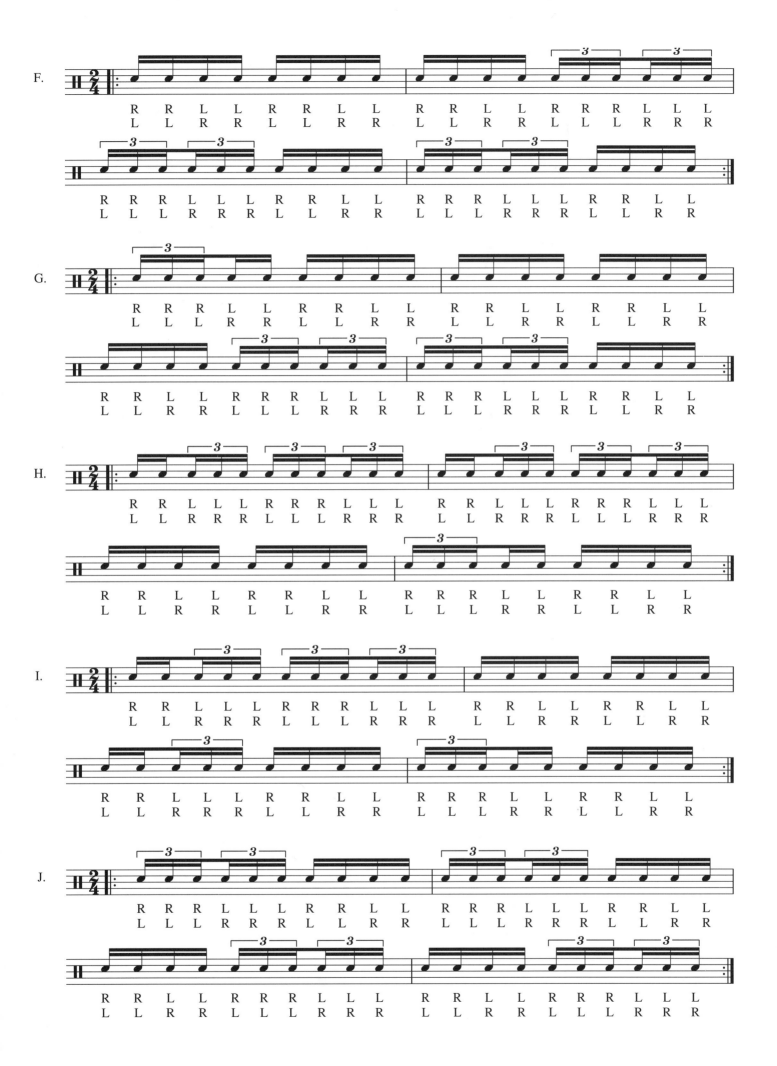

Eight-bar Phrases

The eight-bar exercises are combined phrases based on the triple and double stroke roll rudimental variations. Repeat each phrase until you are comfortable with the different sticking combinations, and then create your own eight-bar phrases.

A.

```
R R L L R R R L L L      R R L L L R R R L L L      R R  R L L  L      R R L L L R R R L L L
L L R R L L L R R R      L L R R L L L R R R      L L  L R R  R      L L L R R L L L R R R
```

```
R R L L R R L L      R R R L L L R R R L L L      R R R L L L      R R L L L R R R L
L L R R L L R R      L L L R R R L L L R R R      L L L R R R      L L R R R L L L R
```

B.

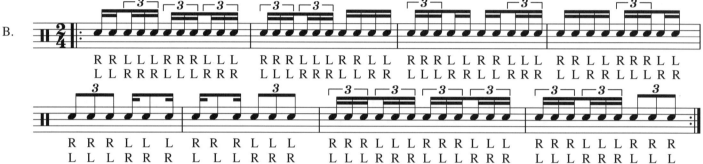

```
R R L L L R R R L L L      R R R L L L R R L L      R R R L L R R L L L      R R L L R R R L L
L L R R R L L L R R R      L L L R R R L L R R      L L L R R L L R R R      L L R R L L L R R
```

```
R R R L L  L      R R  R L L  L      R R R L L L R R R L L L      R R R L L L R R  R
L L L R R  R      L L  L R R  R      L L L R R R L L L R R R      L L L R R R L L  L
```

Bass Drum and Hi-hat Ostinatos

The following bass drum and hi-hat ostinatos can be played underneath the previous triple and double stroke roll rudimental exercises.

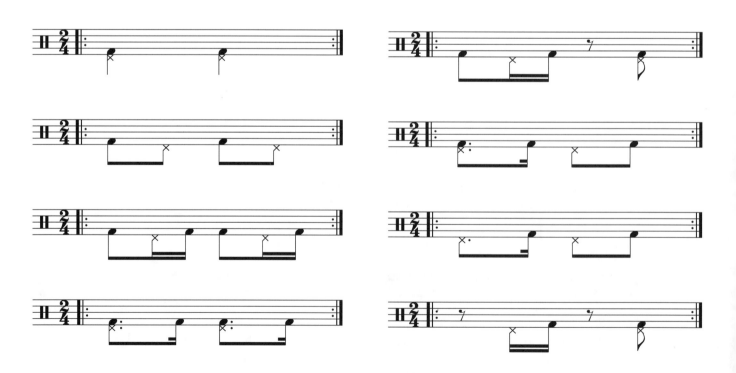

CHAPTER 5: Swiss Army Triple Variations

The following examples are variations based on the *Swiss Army Triple* rudiment. These rudiment variations consist of flams with single, duple, and triple sticking combinations. Utilize a metronome and/or tap your foot as you repeat each exercise until you feel comfortable with the sticking.

Exercises

Four-bar Phrases

The four-bar exercises are combined phrases based on Swiss Army Triplet variations. Repeat each example phrase until you are comfortable with the different sticking combinations, and then create your own four-bar phrases.

Eight-bar Phrases

The eight-bar exercises are combined phrases based on Swiss Army Triplet variations. Repeat each example phrase until you are comfortable with the different sticking combinations, and then create your own eight-bar phrases.

Bass Drum and Hi-hat Ostinatos

The following bass drum and hi-hat ostinatos can be played underneath the previous Swiss Army Triplet exercises.

CHAPTER 6:
Rolls, Tempos, and Rhythmic Pulsations

The following examples show the correlation between tempo and the rhythmic pulsation of rolls. These variations are based on the *long roll* rudiment and consist of duple sticking combinations. The first example illustrates the *long roll*, which can be played at different tempos as shown in the examples that follow. The tempo range for each specific roll is designated with a rhythmic pulsation. Begin by playing the rhythmic pulsation, and then double the sticking to play the *long roll*. Utilize a metronome as you repeat each exercise. The CD demonstrations are played at the fastest tempo shown for each roll.

Long Roll written:

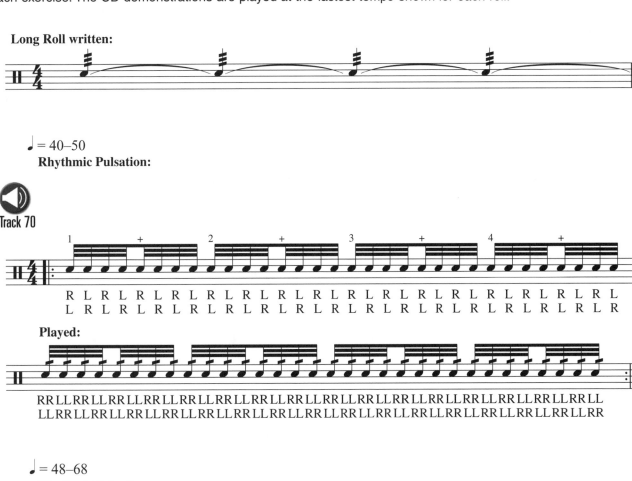

♩ = 40–50
Rhythmic Pulsation:

Track 70

1.

R L R L R L R L R L R L R L R L R L R L R L R L R L R L R L R L
L R L R L R L R L R L R L R L R L R L R L R L R L R L R L R L R

Played:

RR LL RR LL RR LL RR LL RR LL RR LL RR LL RR LL RR LL RR LL RR LL RR LL RR LL RR LL RR LL RR LL
LL RR LL RR LL RR LL RR LL RR LL RR LL RR LL RR LL RR LL RR LL RR LL RR LL RR LL RR LL RR LL RR

♩ = 48–68
Rhythmic Pulsation:

Track 71

2.

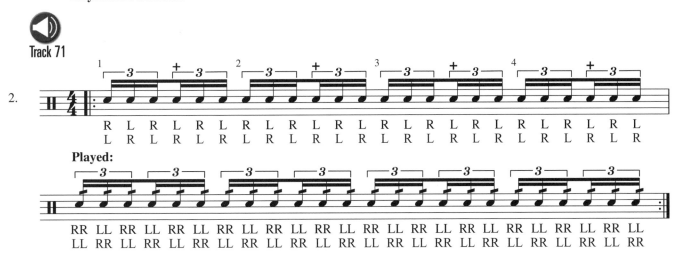

R L R L R L R L R L R L R L R L R L R L R L R L R L R L R L R L
L R L R L R L R L R L R L R L R L R L R L R L R L R L R L R L R

Played:

RR LL RR LL RR LL RR LL RR LL RR LL RR LL RR LL RR LL RR LL RR LL RR LL RR LL
LL RR LL RR LL RR LL RR LL RR LL RR LL RR LL RR LL RR LL RR LL RR LL RR LL RR

♩ = 80–100
Rhythmic Pulsation:

Track 72

3.

Played:

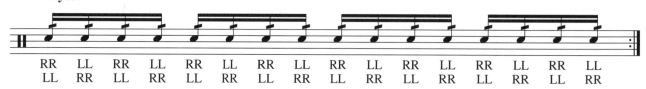

♩ = 150–200
Rhythmic Pulsation:

Track 73

4.

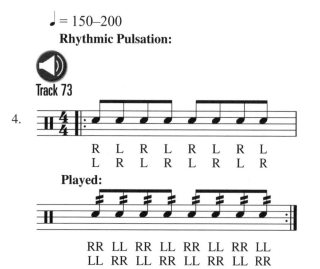

Played:

♩ = 120–140
Rhythmic Pulsation:

Track 74

5.

Played:

Even Roll Exercise

This exercise will help you develop an even roll, which can only be accomplished by pulling the sound out of the snare drum.

Begin by playing a double stroke roll as slow as possible and accent the second stroke of each hand. Increase the tempo as much as possible, and then decrease the tempo back to the original starting point. Each day push to increase the tempo while maintaining accuracy. To help keep track of your progress use a metronome to record your daily maximum tempo. As you increase the tempo, the accents will eventually transform into an even stroke roll.

Hints

- Slower rolls require more stick height motion, while faster rolls require less stick height.

- Do not mash the roll **into** the snare drum head. Instead, pull the roll **out** of the snare drum. This can be accomplished by playing each stroke and quickly lifting the stick *away* from the drumhead—instead of downward and into the drumhead.

- Play all roll exercises with brushes instead of sticks. This will help strengthen the muscles needed to execute a great sounding roll.

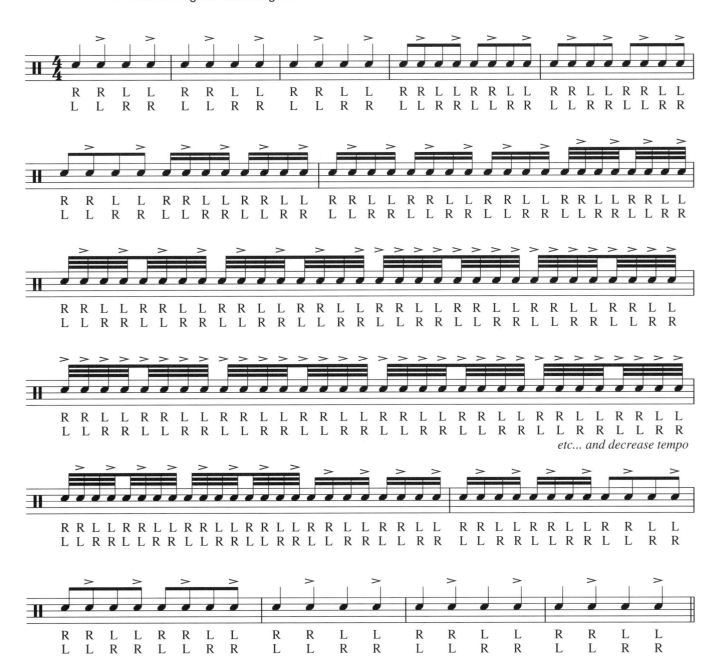

CHAPTER 7: Let's Roll

The following exercises are variations based on the double stroke roll rudiments, including the drag strokes, double stroke, five stroke, six stroke, seven stroke, nine stroke, ten stroke, eleven stroke, thirteen stroke, fifteen stroke, and seventeen stroke roll. Once you're comfortable with the stickings, try the bass drum and hi-hat ostinatos on pages 53 and 58 along with the roll exercises.

4/4 Roll Exercises

These exercises illustrate roll permutations (brackets are shown to indicate roll lengths) using the sixteenth-note pulse in 4/4 time. The pulse reference (first bar) can be omitted or played between each exercise. Repeat or play each bar in succession with or without the pulse reference bar. You also have the option of playing through the 4/4 exercises in succession. It is important to use a metronome and/or tap your foot as you play the following exercises.

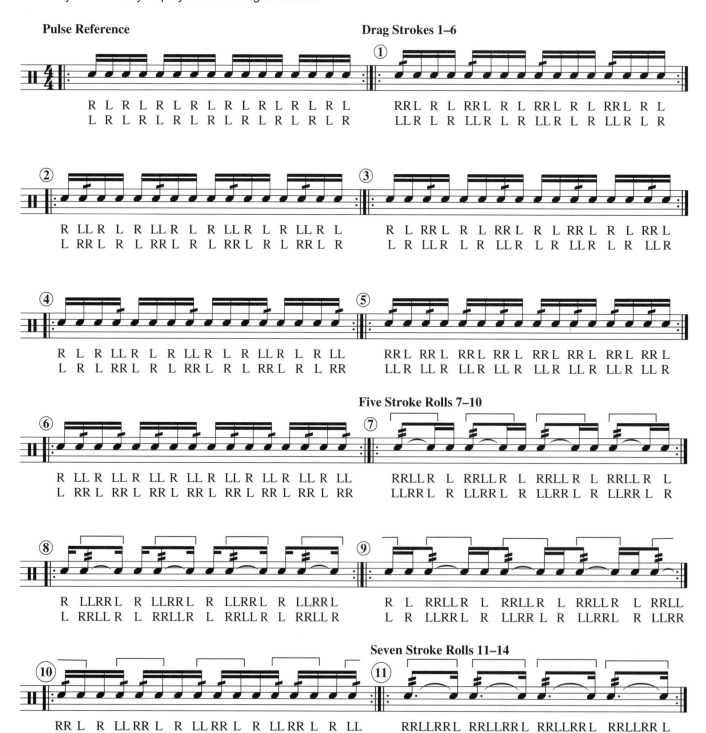

Pulse Reference

Drag Strokes 1–6

Five Stroke Rolls 7–10

Seven Stroke Rolls 11–14

RRLL R LL RRLL R LL RRLL R LL RRLL R LL   RR L RRLL RR L RRLL RR L RRLL RR L RRLL
LLRR L RR LLRR L RR LLRR L RR LLRR L RR   LL R LLRR LL R LLRR LL R LLRR LL R LLRR

Long Roll

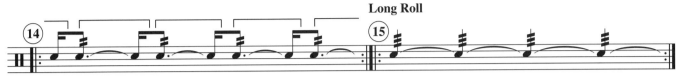

R LLRRLL R LLRRLL R LLRRLL R LLRRLL   RRLLRRLL RRLLRRLL RRLLRRLL RRLLRRLL
L RRLLRR L RRLLRR L RRLLRR L RRLLRR   LLRRLLRR LLRRLLRR LLRRLLRR LLRRLLRR

Nine Stroke Rolls 16–19

RRLLRRLL R L R L RRLLRRLL R L R L   R LLRRLLRR L R L R LLRRLLRR L R L
LLRRLLRR L R L R LLRRLLRR L R L R   L RRLLRRLL R L R L RRLLRRLL R L R

R L RRLL RRLL R L R L RRLL RRLL R L   R L R LL RRLLRRL R L R LL RRLLRRL
L R LLRR LLRR L R L R LLRR LLRR L R   L R L RR LLRRLLR L R L RR LLRRLLR

Ten Stroke Rolls 20–23

RRLLRRLL R L   RRLLRRLL R L   R LLRRLL RR L R   R LLRRLL RR L R
LLRRLLRR L R   LLRRLLRR L R   L RRLLRR LL R L   L RRLLRR LL R L

RRLL RRLL R L   RRLL RRLL R L   R LLRR LLRR L R   LLRR LLRR L
LLRR LLRR L R   LLRR LLRR L R   L RRLL RRLL R L   RRLL RRLL R

Eleven Stroke Rolls 24–27

RRLLRRLLRR L R L RRLLRRLLRR L R L   R LLRRLL RRLL R L R LLRRLL RRLL R L
LLRRLLRRLL R L R LLRRLLRRLL R L R   L RRLLRR LLRR L R L RRLLRR LLRR L R

R L RRLL RRLLRR L R L RRLL RRLLRR L   R L R LL RRLLRRLL R L R LL RRLLRRLL
L R LLRR LLRRLL R L R LLRR LLRRLL R   L R L RR LLRRLLRR L R L RR LLRRLLRR

Thirteen Stroke Rolls 28–31

RRLLRRLL RRLL R L RRLLRRLL RRLL R L   R LLRRLL RRLLRR L R LLRRLL RRLLRR L
LLRRLLRR LLRR L R LLRRLLRR LLRR L R   L RRLLRR LLRRLL R L RRLLRR LLRRLL R

R L RRLL RRLLRRLL R L RRLL RRLLRRLL   RR L R LL RRLLRRLL RR L R LL RRLLRRLL
L R LLRR LLRRLLRR L R LLRR LLRRLLRR   LL R L RR LLRRLLRR LL R L RR LLRRLLRR

Fifteen Stroke Rolls 32–35

RRLLRRLL RRLLRR L RRLLRRLL RRLLRR L   R LLRRLL RRLLRRLL R LLRRLL RRLLRRLL
LLRRLLRR LLRRLL R LLRRLLRR LLRRLL R   L RRLLRR LLRRLLRR L RRLLRR LLRRLLRR

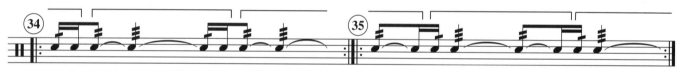

RR L RRLL RRLLRRLL RR L RRLL RRLLRRLL   RRLL R LL RRLLRRLL RRLL R LL RRLLRRLL
LL R LLRR LLRRLLRR LL R LLRR LLRRLLRR   LLRR L RR LLRRLLRR LLRR L RR LLRRLLRR

Seventeen Stroke Rolls 36–39

RRLLRRLL RRLLRRLL R L R L R L R L   R LLRRLL RRLLRRLL RR L R L R L R L
LLRRLLRR LLRRLLRR L R L R L R L R   L RRLLRR LLRRLLRR LL R L R L R L R

R L RRLL RRLLRRLL RRLL R L R L R L   R L R LL RRLLRRLL RRLLRRLL R L R L
L R LLRR LLRRLLRR LLRR L R L R L R   L R L RR LLRRLLRR LLRRLLRR L R L R

4/4 Bass Drum and Hi-hat Ostinatos

The following bass drum and hi-hat ostinatos will add a new and exciting challenge to drumset players. Begin by playing the ostinato of your choosing. Then play the previous roll exercises on top of it.

Hint

Make sure to thoroughly familiarize yourself with the hand exercises before attempting to play them with the ostinatos.

3 + 2 son clave

3 + 2 rumba clave

2 + 3 son clave

2 + 3 rumba clave

6/8 Roll Exercises

These exercises illustrate roll permutations (brackets are shown to indicate roll lengths) using the sixteenth-note pulse in 6/8 time. The pulse reference (first bar) can be omitted or played between each exercise. Repeat or play each bar in succession with or without the pulse reference bar. You also have the option of playing through the 6/8 exercises in succession. It is important to use a metronome and/or tap your foot as you play the following exercises.

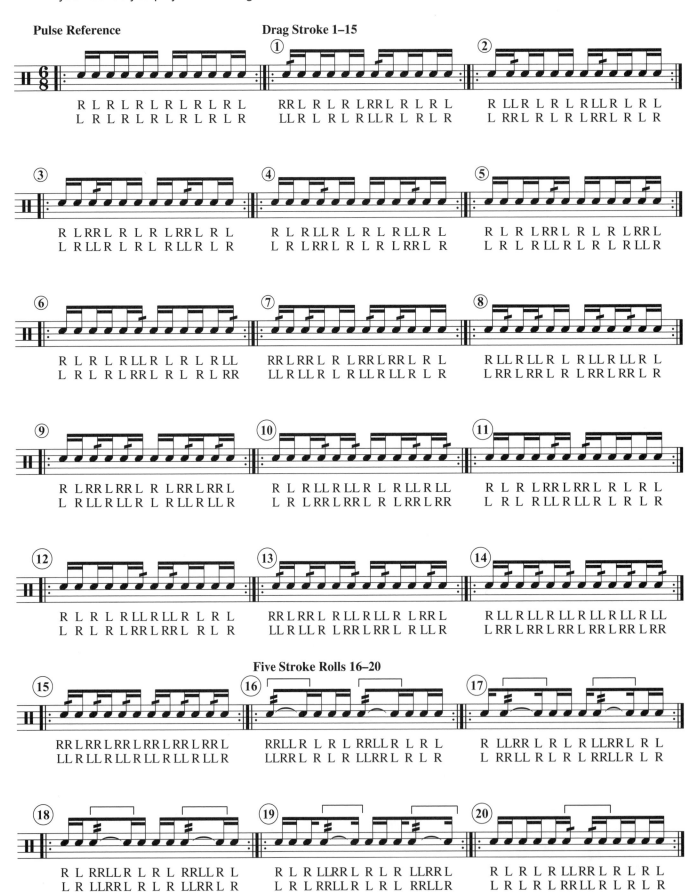

Pulse Reference

R L R L R L R L R L R L
L R L R L R L R L R L R

Drag Stroke 1–15

① RRL R L R L RRL R L R L
LL R L R L R LL R L R L R

② R LL R L R L RLL R L R L
L RRL R L R L RRL R L R

③ R L RRL R L R L RRL R L
L R LL R L R L RLL R L R

④ R L RLL R L R L RLL R L
L R LRRL R L R L RRL R

⑤ R L R LRRL R L R L RRL
L R L RLL R L R L RLL R

⑥ R L R L RLL R L R L RLL
L R L R LRRL R L R L RR

⑦ RRLRRL R L RRL RRL R L
LL R LL R L R LL R LL R L R

⑧ R LL R LL R L R LL R LL R L
L RRL RRL R L RRL RRL R

⑨ R LRRL RRL R L RRL RRL
L RLL R LL R L RLL R LL R

⑩ R L RLL R LL R L R LL R LL
L R LRRL RRL R L RRL RR

⑪ R L R LRRL RRL R L R L
L R L RLL R LL R L R L R

⑫ R L R L RLL R LL R L R L
L R L R L RRL RRL R L R

⑬ RRLRRL R LL R LL R LRRL
LL R LL R LRRL RRL R LL R

⑭ R LL R LL R LL R LL R LL R LL
L RRL RRL R L RRL RRL RR

⑮ RRL RRL RRL RRL RRL RRL
LL R LL R LL R LL R LL R LL R

Five Stroke Rolls 16–20

⑯ RRLL R L R L RRLL R L R L
LLRRL R L R L LLRRL R L R

⑰ R LLRR L R L R LLRRL R L
L RRLL R L R L RRLL R L R

⑱ R L RRLL R L R L RRLL R L
L R LLRRL R L R L LLRRL R

⑲ R L R LLRR L R L R LLRRL
L R L RRLL R L R L RRLL R

⑳ R L R L RLLRR L R L R L
L R L R L RRLL R L R L R

Seven Stroke Rolls 21–25

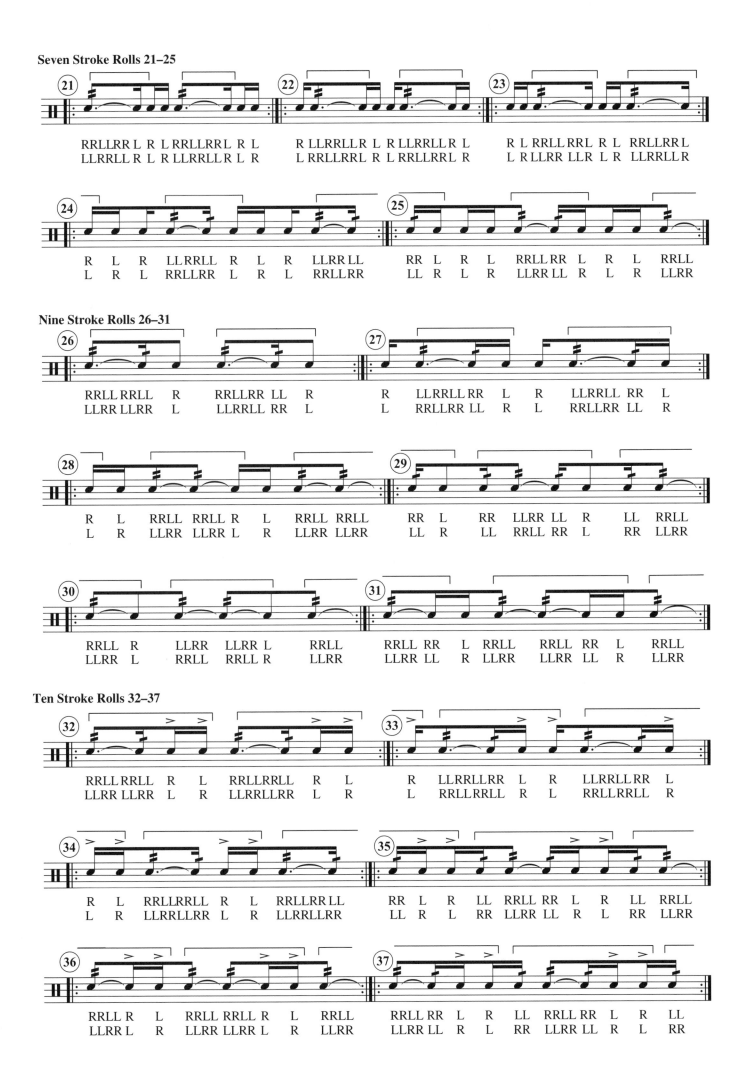

Nine Stroke Rolls 26–31

Ten Stroke Rolls 32–37

Eleven Stroke Rolls 38–43

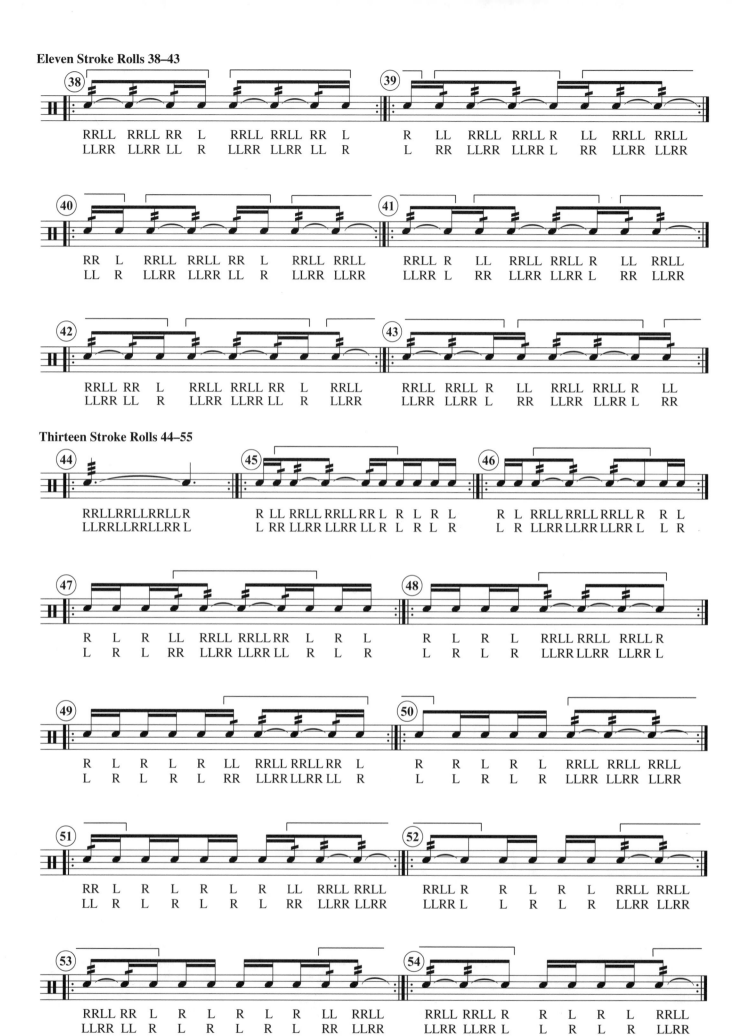

Thirteen Stroke Rolls 44–55

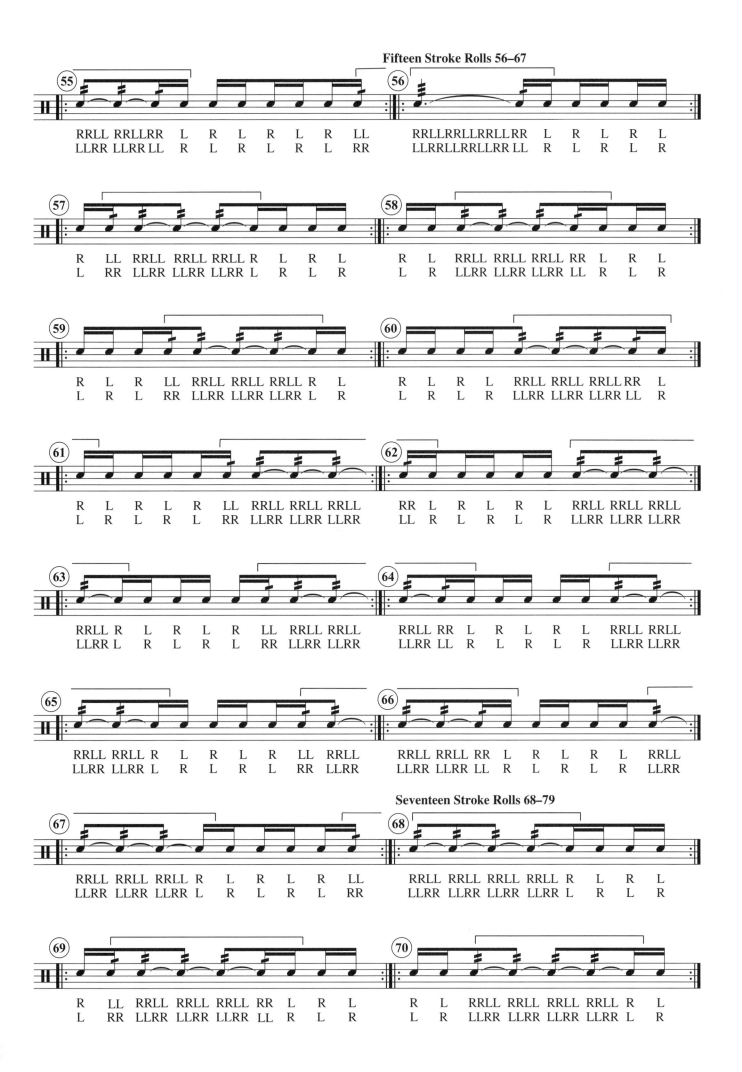

Long Roll

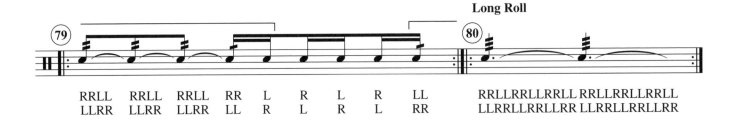

6/8 Bass Drum and Hi-hat Ostinatos

The following bass drum and hi-hat ostinatos will add a new and exciting challenge to drumset players. Begin by playing the ostinato of your choosing. Then play the previous roll rudiment exercises on top of it.

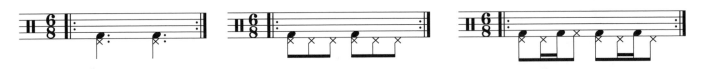

CHAPTER 8: Rudimental Solos

The following solos are based on the rudimental warm-up exercises in the book. Play each solo until you're comfortable with the sticking before adding the suggested drumset ostinatos. The solos and drumset ostinatos are written in 4/4, 6/8, 2/4, and 3/4 time signatures. Always use a metronome and/or tap your foot as you play the following solos. All the rudimental solos are demonstrated as written on the CD.

Solo 1

Solo 2

Bass Drum and Hi-hat Ostinatos

3 + 2 son clave

3 + 2 rumba clave

2 + 3 son clave

2 + 3 rumba clave

Solo 3

Solo 4

Bass Drum and Hi-hat Ostinatos

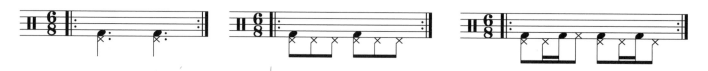

Solo 5

Solo 6

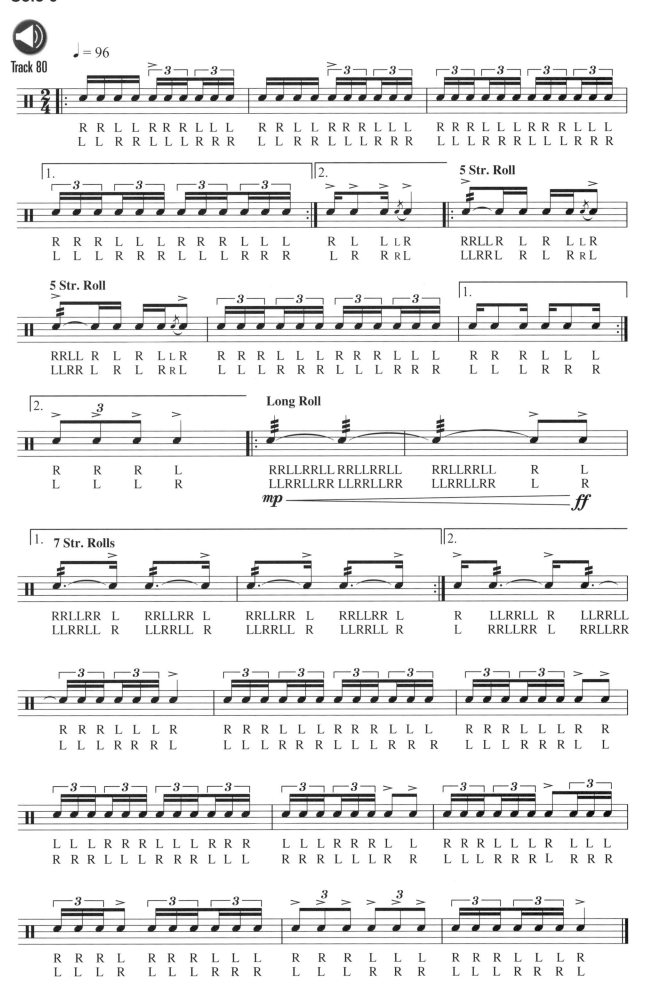

Bass Drum and Hi-hat Ostinatos

Solo 7

Solo 8

Bass Drum and Hi-hat Ostinatos

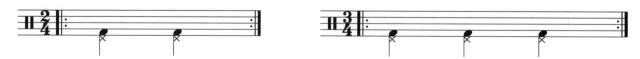

EQUIPMENT USED

Pearl Drums

Sensitone Classic 14x5 Steel Shell Snare Drum featuring a beaded shell with a vintage-look and chrome-plated solid brass tube lugs. The drum has the SuperHoop II Rims and solid brass tension rods. The Sensitone Classic provides a smooth, neutral, and well-balanced sound with excellent attack and projection, combined with outstanding body and tonal clarity.

Ultra Cast Series 14x5 Snare Drum. The milled cast aluminum shell snare drum has precision cut bearing edges that make tuning easy with perfect head seating around the circumference of the drum. The Ultra Cast features an all black lacquered coated shell, tube lugs, and SuperHoop II Rims. The drum provides the warm, round, full bodied tone of a wood shell but has all the crack, volume, and projection needed.

BRX 14x6.5 Master Studio Snare Drum. This drum features 6 ply birch 7.5mm shells, producing crisper, almost "metal-like", highs for superb presence and articulation. The drum features the MasterCast die cast hoops, bridge lugs, SR-017 vertical-pull strainer, and ultra-precise Stainless Steel tension rods and brass receivers.

Master Custom Extra (20 inch) Bass Drum featuring D-054 claws with rubber gaskets to protect the beauty of the hoops. Recessed tension rod receivers prevent accidental tension changes for set-and-forget tuning. The bass drums are offered in standard and power depths in diameters ranging from 18 to 24 inches. Standard features include SP-30 spurs, BB-3 bass bracket, and Remo Powerstroke3 bass drum heads.

Remo Heads

Ambassador heads are medium-weighted heads made with a single-ply 10mil film to produce an open, bright, and resonant sound with plenty of attack.

Paiste Signature Series Cymbals

The 13 inch Dark crisp Hi-Hats' sound character can be described as fairly dark, full, and crisp with a pronounced stick sound. They produce a lively, medium sustain with a full, tight chick sound. These hi-hats are versatile, consist of medium thin top/extra heavy bottom, and can be played soft to loud volumes.

E-Pad! Practice Pad

The circular pad (EP12) has an Enduraflex playing surface that can be used directly on a snare drum as a single practice pad or placed on a stand. E-pads are great for situations where high intensity and low volume are desired. The ProDeluxe kneepad offers the benefit of anywhere, anytime convenience. Great for all styles of playing—from beginner to pro!

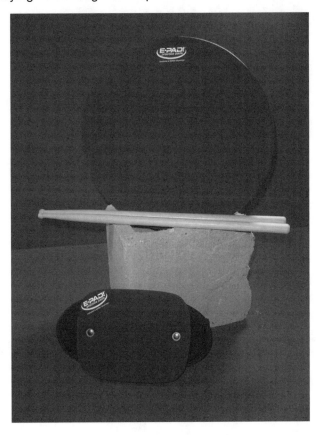

Regal Tip Sticks

8A 208R (.555" x 16") wood tip lacquered stick that amazingly resists slippage and is perfectly balanced. The 8A is a versatile stick that can be used to play at loud or soft volumes. Regal Tip offers a variety of tip shapes and sizes to create an endless array of sound possibilities on drums and cymbals.

8A
208R (.555" x 16")